Amnesiac Killer : The True Story of Danielle Stewart

Les Ackerman

Published by Trellis Publishing, 2021.

AMNESIAC KILLER : THE TRUE STORY OF DANIELLE STEWART

First edition. June 30, 2021.

Written by Les Ackerman.

AMNESIAC KILLER : THE TRUE STORY OF DANIELLE STEWART

LES ACKERMAN

"I would punish all of those who had never lost anything, those who had never had anything taken away from them. I would let the anger from my chest reach out and explode in spectacular violence." - An excerpt from a poem by Danielle Stewart

Danielle Stewart had a normal and happy childhood until around the age of seven. Both of her parents were public servants and the family lived in the Curtin, Canberra region of Australia. She had one younger sister and the family seemed en route to living a normal, happy life.

Danielle was particularly close to her father during her childhood years. He took her swimming, read books to her at night and sang to her. She described him as being a man with a great sense of humor and the kind of man who "did all the things that dads do."

At the age of seven, however, Danielle's life took a traumatic turn. Her family was building a holiday house in the NSW south coast town of Batemans Bay. Danielle, unfortunately, came into the cross hairs of a sexual predator.

The man was a neighbor and Danielle would come over to his home to watch TV as they had no television of their own in their holiday house. The man was a married real estate agent in his 50s. He would let Danielle and a friend come with him to outings where they would examine unoccupied houses he was selling. It was there, inside these homes, that the assaults would take place.

Danielle would be under the man's spell for over three years before they molestations came to an end.

When she was eleven years old, tragedy struck again in the form of losing her mother to cancer. Distraught, her father sent her away for a weekend with a friend of a family. The family had a teenaged son, however, who constantly harassed Danielle, molesting her as well.

Her father would remarry six months later to a woman who had three children of her own. Danielle felt betrayed by her father's remarriage and tried to commit suicide with an overdose of pills. Her father himself had suffered from depression and fell apart emotionally after the death of Danielle's mother.

"I've always believed that depression and mental illness is inheritable," forensic psychologist Pauline Malloy said. "Sometimes through genetics, sometimes through thought processes. With Danielle, she clearly inherited some mental illness from her father's side of the family as her dad suffered from depression as well as her paternal grandfather."

Her maternal grandparents arrived and offered that Danielle come live with them. Danielle didn't want to go, she wanted to stay with her Dad but her father didn't want her screwing up the dynamics of his new family with her bad behavior.

He wanted her gone.

So Danielle was given two choices, either go live with her grandparents or go to a youth shelter.

Danielle chose to run away

"Danielle suffered numerous traumas, back to back," Malloy said. "The loss of her innocence, the loss of her mom and then the rejection of her father. Any of the above could have been cause for life altering psychological trauma but she suffered all of these within a four year time span. It had to crush her psychically and she did not have the life experience to cope."

Running away, the twelve year old girl roughed it out on the streets. Finally, she grew tired and returned home to her father. She would not be treated as the prodigal daughter, however, as her father had her bags packed and waiting. He drove Danielle to a local youth shelter and dropped her off.

Danielle would remain there for the next three months.

Danielle did not like the youth refuge. There was a lot of drug use, alcohol and she once again experienced sexual abuse.

"This was a horrid life for her at this point," Malloy said. "At some point I think she broke down psychologically and the seeds for future violent behavior were planted here."

RETURNING HOME

She eventually returned home to live with her father but he had settled in with his new family.

"I felt so alone, unloved, misunderstood," Danielle recalled. "and as the problems at home got worse, I got worse. I was sneaking out of the house, drinking, drugging. I missed my mum so terribly, I just wanted to be with her."

Danielle would attempt suicide on several occasions, leaving permanent scars on her wrist.

"I used a razor in my bedroom downstairs," Danielle said. "There was no internet back then and I didn't know how to do it [properly]."

On her 13th birthday, her father celebrated by throwing her out of the house once again. She would go and live with her friend Elle O'Brien and her mother. O'Brien's mother fed her and took her in, allowing the unwanted girl to remain there for four years.

At the age of sixteen, she enrolled at Narrabundah College and become a student of renowned poet Geoff Page.

"She was leagues ahead of anyone I've encountered writing contemporary poetry at that age," Page recalled. "She had some of the same virtues as Sylvia Plath, a real feeling for adventurous imagery. There was a lot going on in her brain at an intense level and she had the talent to turn it into something moving."

Under the guidance of her teacher, Danielle published an anthology of poems called "I for Icarus."

Danielle would go on to study performing arts at Melbourne's Monash University before traveling to Sydney to share an apartment with her step-sister, Myfanwy Thompson. Both young women would indulge in alcohol and prescription drugs, becoming the catalyst for each others self-destructive behavior. Myfanwy, however, would suffer a freak accident in falling off a cliff while taking ecstasy.

The loss devastated Danielle as she considered Myfanwy to be her best friend.

"Her boyfriend had got into dealing ecstasy," Danielle said. "I couldn't handle seeing her wasted all the time, so I'd moved out with other friends."

Her younger step-brother, Tristram would later die of an aneurysm after being diagnosed with schizophrenia.

MEANDERING THROUGH LIFE

Danielle was now 24 and wandered aimlessly through life. She went from one job to the next until she met the 50-year old Chaim Kimel in late 2000.

"They met on the dance floor and hit it off immediately," journalist Byron Kaye said.

Despite the age difference, Chaim Kamel was a stylish man with his own business.

"He was a bit of a bon vivant," crime author Paul Kidd said. "Lived in the good part of Sydney. A good lifestyle."

"He was very charismatic, very gregarious, very charming, very generous, strong and creative," Danielle said. "He loved his children and they loved him."

Kimel had been a successful entrepreneur, dealing in antiques. She got a job working for Chaim in his furniture store, Eclectica in Mosman. Kimel had put Danielle in charge of bookkeeping.

The two got along exceptionally well, at first, with common interests in art, music, and food.

"Danielle was a very attractive," Kidd said. "Petite, blonde, loved to drink. He (Chaim) was an older man but a really good style of a bloke."

The relationship started platonic in the beginning.

"He made some advances which weren't initially reciprocated," Kaye said. "But over time, they became intimate and it was on."

Kimel thought Danielle was a "prize catch". He invited Danielle over to visit his family and she was impressed with how close and living they were. There she saw, for the first time since her early childhood, a loving family that she could be a part of.

Danielle moved in with Kimel who had the time lived with his ten year old son Jordan. He also had a daughter, Amber and Fred, who were in their early twenties and late teens respectively.

A CHANGE IN DEMEANOR?

One of her friends, however, thought that Danielle changed after she met Chaim. She described him as being very possessive and told her what to do.

"I loved him," Danielle said. "I still do. It is a love-hate thing and it won't ever go. With those types of personalities, there is that level of attention, you become their entire focus."

Danielle would have these kind of intense relationships all of her life and it seemed to be the fuel to her fire. She was irresistibly drawn to the drama and would have it on full blast with Chaim Kimel.

"Anyone who would have been in a relationship with Danielle Stewart would have been in a relationship that was doomed from the start," Kidd said. "The combination of psychological problems fueled by excesses of alcohol was always going to end in disaster."

COCAINE AND BOOZE

Danielle began substance abuse at an early age which only progressed as she got older. She now had a benefactor in Chaim as well as an enabler as he liked to party, indulging in cocaine himself.. He didn't realize, however, that the alcohol would only stoke the flames that would extinguish their relationship.

He also had a dark side, according to Danielle's grandmother. She described him as someone who was "demanding and overpowering."

"She (Danielle) went through life with a paranoia that people were going to leave her," Kidd said. "And she became very, very possessive of her partner and that fueled by alcohol was the basis of the majority of their problems."

CALL THE POLICE

Once the relationship turned intimate, things started getting out of hand. The two indulged in alcohol and had numerous fights in which the police were called in.

Danielle had been taking strong anti-depression medications and mixing these drugs with alcohol. One fight had gotten so severe that she took a restraining order out against Kimel.

On one occasion, Kimel violated the order and was jailed for one night.

"I'd moved into temporary accommodation and Chaim came after me," Danielle said. "He broke into my room and stole my laptop and wallet. The police busted him on the way out and took him to jail for the night."

Kimel explained to the police that he violated the order because Danielle had called him stating that she had swallowed fourteen Valiums.

"I'm fine when I'm not in an emotional situation," Danielle said, "but when I'm under threat, the flashbacks can be extreme."

"She (Danielle) had a borderline personality disorder," Malloy said. "When things go bad with her, they go real bad. That was how she lived her entire life up until that point. She had to engage in fights, drinking, drugs. Drama, drama, drama. If it isn't there, she will create it."

A PROPENSITY FOR VIOLENCE

Kimel's son, Jordan, was ten years old when his father first met Danielle. He recalled Danielle as a destructive psychotic stating that she would "cut up $10,000 worth of business suits, delete important documents from my father's computer. Once, she punched through a glass bathroom window and slashed her wrists. And she'd punch my father, too."

"Unfortunately, this was the pattern that was set," Malloy set. "They would argue, fight and then get back together. When they would get back together things would be more passionate and clingy than before. 'Please, don't leave me,' that sort of thing. But then the cycle repeats itself and it has to be more extreme in order for the couple to get that same 'high.'"

The couple would remain together and make attempts to appear respectable. In 2004, Danielle enrolled at a nearby college to finish her degree while they both started an online catering company called Epicurean. The money to start the company was borrowed from Danielle's grandmother, a total of $30,000.

Later that year, the couple would journey to India where they would marry at the Taj Mahal.

Danielle would claim, however, that the money the borrowed for the business is what kept her in the marriage .

"Part of the reason I married Chaim was because I was worried about my grandparents' money," Danielle said. "If I left him, there'd be no legal recourse for me to get it back. He took it without shame; he never planned to pay it back."

"Typical of people with borderline personality disorders," Malloy said. "Is that they have to play the role of the victim. It is a head scratcher as to why Chaim would borrow thirty-grand when he had his own business. Maybe he thought he would be placating her somehow with them being in business together and having her feel as if she were a part of things. But clearly he didn't need anything more on his plate."

BOOMERANG BABY

Danielle would leave Kimel a total of seven times during their seven year relationship. She would confide in her grandmother and friend Elle, saying she was unhappy. Then he would call and they would get back together.

"It (their relationship) was very alcohol fueled," Kaye said. "Very hedonistic. A lot of violent arguments."

Danielle blamed her inability to stay away from Chaim on her lack of self-esteem.

"While he could be caring, it was undermined by his desire to keep me enslaved to him," Danielle said. "When I left him, he'd follow me and get me back. When your sense of self-esteem is so low and a learnt helplessness has set in, you don't feel able to support yourself. My friends had dropped off because they couldn't stand him. The only times I responded with violence were when I was trying to leave and he'd try to stop me. He'd hide my wallet, phone, computer, passport. Those times always ended with me being in hospital, not him. I never tried to kill him: I tried to kill myself."

WHO WAS ABUSING WHO?

It became apparent to Kimel's family, however, that he had married a woman prone to violent outbursts. Kimel told his daughter than Danielle had bitten him on his thumb and arm as as smashing his glasses.

He had his glasses broken so much that it had become a "running joke", according to his daughter Amber.

After arguments, Danielle would delete Kimel's emails and computer files. Kimel had became so enraged at her actions that he kicked her out of the house. Danielle would return, kicking out the timber door.

WELCOME TO THE PSYCH WARD

Danielle had overdosed on medication numerous times during the course of her marriage. She would inform doctors that Kimel was controlling and that she had "nothing to live for."

His daughter, Amber, however, expressed concern for her father's well being and wanted him to sever ties with Danielle.

"He told me he'd made a commitment to be there for her and loved her unconditionally," Amber said. "He was convinced unconditional love would cure her."

"Chaim was the rescuer," Malloy said. "He couldn't help himself. Danielle was the beautiful damsel in distress. They had passionate sex together, he knew about her past, and he couldn't be another man that brought more pain in her life. He didn't want that. He thought that through his own sincerity and love that he could somehow bring her to a place of healing. But he wasn't a professional. And that isn't what relationships are for."

A NEW MAN

In 2006, Danielle separated from Kimel and met Melbourne university professor Joeri Mol. She moved in with him and became pregnant by December of that year. Danielle wanted to go back to Sydney, however, and didn't want to raise the child with Mol as a single mother.

"She went out with somebody else," Kaye said. "He was seeing other people but they could not stop speaking. They remained extremely close. The new fellow (Mol) wants to settle down and start raising a family. Which incidentally was Danielle's greatest dream, which was to have a family. But she's still drawn to Chaim uncontrollably."

A week later, she called Kimel and the two met to discuss a reconciliation.

"He (Chaim) told her that either she as a termination," Kidd said. "Or there's no hope if them ever getting back together."

She complied with his request, her second abortion in six months (the first with Kimel) and she once again went into a depression.

"Danielle desperately wanted to experience the happiness that she had before her mother died," Malloy said. "She always told her grandmother, 'I just want have a normal life. I just want to have a normal life.' What she really wanted was that family again. So now she spends her life grasping at straws, going from this man to that man, and getting multiple abortions."

BURNING THE CANDLE AT BOTH ENDS

The couple moved back in together in 2007 but this time their break-up would be much more volatile.

And violent.

"It was short lived (their reconciliation)," Kidd said. "Now that they were back together. It was business as usual."

Business as usual was a lot of fighting and alcohol coupled with a flurry of activity to keep up with the bills.

Danielle returned to college and continued to run their catering business, The Epicurean. In order to make ends meet, however, she took a part time job at a Sydney ad agency.

She couldn't juggle all of these things at once, so she turned to cocaine and alcohol. Her friends described her as "withdrawn" and "unsettled" after meeting with her after the latest reconciliation.

Danielle began to feel the itch to run away again, telling friends she now just wanted to earn some money on her own and get away from Kimel for good.

"How the hell could this have worked to begin with?" Malloy said. "You've got a woman with some serious issues, abused by men, abandoned as a child and now she's an alcoholic with major depression. The pattern is set in their relationship. Break-up, get back together, fight some more. Rinse and repeat. This can only end badly. The question was, how bad?"

THE FATEFUL DINNER

"The old problems kept resurfacing," Kaye said. "They kept on with the dinner parties. Living the good life. And with this came Danielle's terrible response to alcohol access."

On August 23rd of 2007, Danielle went out with Kimel to have dinner at a restaurant called Pescador. They were described in a police statement by their friend, Angela Batley, to be in "good spirits."

"It is noted by others there that Danielle seemed a little drunker than usual," Kaye said. "Things got a little bit more testy and Danielle left and decided to walk home."

After dinner, Chaim went with his friends to Angela Batley's home. He would call Danielle from the home and she said that she would come and pick him up. Things took a turn for the strange when Danielle came over but drove back without Chaim who ended up walking home.

Batley was concerned about the tenseness of the situation and called Kimel to make sure he got home safe. Kimel told Batley that Danielle was working on the computer but was "drunk" and that he had to go.

Danielle arrived at their home before Kimel. She told the 16-year old Jordan that she "shouldn't have gone to Angela's house. I've had too much to drink."

Jordan stated that Danielle began playing loud music through the computer, dancing with a drink in her hand. When Kimel arrived, he told her to turn the music down before the neighbors start complaining. An argument ensued before Kimel turned off Danielle's music himself. The argument escalated, the topics being the loud music then escalating to the fact that Chaim would change the password on the computer, which was an ongoing issue in their relationship.

She started to physically attack him but Chaim easily evaded the rushes of the drunk Danielle. Then in the heat of the moment, she picked up one of Chaim's antique ornamental knives he had on display. Chaim came forward, ordering her to place the knife down, then she stuck it into his stomach.

Chaim fell to the ground and she stabbed him again.

"They were both yelling for about 15 minutes," stated Jordan. "All of a sudden, I could hear them in the corridor outside my room. It sounded like someone was being hit or punched and I heard my father say, 'Why are you being violent and attacking me?' They kept fighting and I heard Danielle fall to the floor and scream. Soon after this, I heard my father say in a tense voice, 'What are you doing? Are you crazy?' I heard my father scream three times. I saw [his] white shirt was covered in blood all up the left side from underneath his ribs towards the middle of his torso. Danielle was standing about two metres away and she had our antique knife in her hand."

Jordan saw his father struggling to get to the front door. He was covered in blood and Danielle was hysterical, holding up the knife.

"So the son runs out of his room," Kaye said. "He finds his father clutching his stomach where he's been stabbed twice. Covered in blood. Barely able to speak."

Jordan then thought about attacking Danielle himself.

"He picks up a golf club then thinks for a moment, that he might avenge his father," Kaye said. "It's actually Chaim himself who tells him don't do it. Lying there, sort of holding himself together. The son puts the golf club down and nurses his father while he lies there dying."

Kimel would be rushed to the hospital but die on the operating table at St. Vincent's Hospital, bleeding to death from the two stab wounds to his stomach.

"To the end of his life," Malloy said. "Kimel was protecting Danielle. When his son wanted revenge, he held him back."

Danielle was arrested but plead not guilty on the grounds of self defense. Her blood alcohol reading, however, was five times the legal driving limit.

"It was a stupid, pointless, uncontrolled lover's argument," Kaye said. "And one split second decision led to this terrible outcome."

Danielle maintained no recollection of the events, as she mixed the anti-psychotic drug Seroquel with alcohol. She awoke in a prison cell and called out for her husband, seeing her name on the board with the word 'Murder' written next to it.

"It was the worst moment of my life," Danielle recalled. "In one instant, my entire life had changed and Chaim's had ended."

"Something was going to happen that night," Malloy said. "Her mind was on edge. This may not have been pre-meditated but she knew what was going to happen when she picked up that knife. Remember, she didn't just slash at him as a warning. She thrust the knife into Chaim. Not once. But twice. There was an untapped rage there that came to the surface at the moment. It had been bubbling for a long, long time and unfortunately Chaim Kimel could not foresee how this would end."

THE AFTERMATH

Danielle made a recorded phone call to her father a few days after the killing.

"If I could swap Chaim with me right now, I would do it immediately," Danielle said. "There is no way I meant to kill him."

"Again, I don't think the murder was pre-planned," Malloy said. "But it did seem to be part of Danielle's destiny. What we see here in her killing of Chaim was a metaphor of her own trauma. She was abused by a man in his fifties, molested by him from the ages of seven through ten. She grows into a beautiful woman can choose just about whatever man she wants but instead she elects a man in his fifties, over twenty-five years her senior. That is no coincidence. She is repeating her trauma from the past. But this time she wants to control it. She wants to exorcise the demons of the past so all of those violent fights are trial runs until finally she reaches for that knife and stabs Chaim, metaphorically killing the molester of her past. Now her husband, who actually really loved her, is the victim of this cycle of abuse that has finally come full circle."

Her father agreed to post Danielle's bail but would not agree to the 24-hour surveillance condition attached to it. Her father abandoning her yet again, she turned to her friend Elle O'Brien's mother. She came to bail out Danielle and secured her release after nine months.

Danielle then went to live with her grandmother.

Facing twenty-five years in prison, Danielle would attempt suicide two more times, one of them involving an overdose of Seroquel.

"When I took that Seroquel, I went into psychosis," Danielle said. "It was an out-of-body experience where I thought the nurses were talking about me even though they weren't. I was watching myself from afar. It was crazy, crazy shit. I am sure that is what must have happened on the night Chaim died."

"The psych med plus alcohol defense has become a cliched defense for a lot of killers," Malloy said. "Danielle had done her research. She had studied scriptwriting in school. Everything she said and did had a rehearsed feel to it."

FROM MURDER TO MANSLAUGHTER

The murder charge had been downgraded to manslaughter as Danielle maintained she had no recollection of what happened. She did not remember any of the events of what happened that night not to mention taking the ornamental knife and stabbing her husband with it.

She did not take the stand, however.

"Danielle was charged with murder," Kaye said. "She wept throughout much of the trial. It was very clear that she regretted what she'd done and she wanted him back and she felt quite horrible."

Kimel's children, however, saw Danielle as an imposter the more they investigated the case. They found a synopsis of a play that Danielle had been working on. In the story, one of the characters had a secret desire to kill her older husband.

Fred Kimel, Chaim's oldest son, noted that the play contained details on "jail architecture, prisoner psychology, different cell classifications, prisoner attire, prison visiting hours and life sentences."

The Kimel family once enamored with Danielle, now saw her in a completely different light.

"It was a university assignment, a book I was writing," Danielle said. "I heard that somewhere men kill their partners because they want them to stay, whereas women kill their partners because they want to escape. I know why I was writing about prison: because I was imprisoned long before I was [actually] incarcerated."

SENTENCING

Danielle would be sentenced to six years in prison. She would serve only four.

"There's no doubt that jail saved me," Danielle said. "It prevented me from harming myself with alcohol and drugs. I wouldn't recommend it, though."

During the first nine months of her term, she had been housed in the mental health unit. She could not stop crying. But the prison assigned her to a job in the kitchen and she found her fellow inmates to be helpful.

"I managed to get a few of the heavies on side somehow and avoided the others where possible," Danielle said. "I learnt to assimilate, to hide the fact that I was pretty and educated. I adapted where I could. In jail, I lost everything that made me me: my family, dog, business, house, studies, friends, freedom, clothes, make-up, choices. All I had was myself, my mind and my heart. I learnt to spot evil from a mile away - and evil does exist, I've come face to face with it - but I could still love. This is how I got through jail. Yes, I learnt how to operate within the system, but I could still see beauty in people, and I tried to speak to that."

"Danielle was a well-spoken, educated young woman," Malloy said. "But why the hell would she plead not guilty? She did her research on prison culture beforehand so a cynic can argue that she got off very, very light for what she did. Call it misandry, call it getting the female pass, Danielle was able to get off light for a cold-blooded murderer. She used all of the things from her past to mitigate her own culpability. Sexual abuse, parental death and abandonment down to psych meds and alcohol. She combined those things to get sympathy from Chaim and later from the her jury of her crime."

Danielle walked out of prison on June 24th, 2010.

She is now focused on the prospect of moving to Spain and becoming a professional writer.

"I've paid for what has happened and I've done all I can to fix the issues within myself that contributed to Chaim's death," Danielle said. "I see both a psychiatrist and a psychologist, both of my own volition, nothing to do with parole directives. I don't drink. I don't take drugs. I take responsibility for my actions. I write when I can. I try to love my friends and family. I try to see beauty in the world and I'd like to hope, one day, that I can contribute to that beauty. Still, I love. I still love Chaim. I still love my father. In the end, love will be all I have."

TWISTED SISTERS : THE TRUE STORY OF REGINA AND MARGARET DEFRANCISCO

KORI MAYER

CHAPTER ONE

Regina and Margaret DeFrancisco are two sisters convicted of first degree murder.

On paper, the two sisters look like two girls you would see at a church social.

In school, both were good but not great students. Margaret was the pretty one. She would get all of the attention from the boys but return little interest.

Margaret was a student at Jones College Prep School, a selective public institution that is considered one of the top high schools in Illinois.

A little on the shy side, Margaret had a quick wit and sense of humor. Sweet-looking and pretty, she had avoided any kind of trouble throughout her young life. Her early photos suggest, however, that her subtle smirk was a couldn't contain the narcissism that was growing within.

"You would look at Margaret and see right through her," one of her neighbors said. "It was black, like was nothing there. She didn't seem like she had depth, like she had compassion."

Regina had a love for animals, particularly ponies. She rode horses and in her words, "never lost a show."

Regina was also the more extroverted of the two, wearing her emotions on her sleeve. She could mouth off and had a chip on her shoulder. She also had a thing for 'bad boys', seeing them as a reflection of herself.

"A lot of girls get turned on by the 'thug life'," forensic psychologist Marnie Clark said. "The DeFrancisco sisters definitely fit that mold. They were not out to play Mrs. Cleaver when they grew up. They were attracted to the gang lifestyle. They thought the drama was exciting."

The girls were raised by a single parent, Nora DeFrancisco. Nora raised the two sisters and their brother Joey in the Pilsen neighborhood of Chicago. Their father, Augie DeFrancisco was a small-time burglar and convicted drug dealer who had no involvement in the girl's childhood years. Their maternal grandfather, Gilbert Smith, was a former Chicago cop who was fired from the force in 1960 after admitting that he was "friendly with certain burglars."

Growing up in Pilsen, however, the girls could not avoid rubbing shoulders with gang members. They became enamored with gang culture, learning who fought against who and what the names of the gangs were. There were the Latin Counts, Kool Gang, Villa Lobos, Bishops, among many other offshoots. The girls knew what streets signified what gang members' territory and memorized their hand signals.

"Chicago is simply rife with gangs," Clark said. "It is inescapable, even to those in the more affluent communities. There is still a choice, however. For whatever reason, the DeFrancisco sisters were drawn to the 'thug life'. To a young person, it looks 'cool'.

They are the classic examples of young women who could not see the big picture and thought the thug life was something worth aspiring to."

The two sisters, with their striking brunette looks, could not help but come into the cross hairs of the local gang members. They began wearing dark lipstick and teasing their hair out. Margaret would get a tattoo on her belly. Regina would have the letter "R" tattooed on her leg as well as a drawing of a heart just above her breast. They would hang out on street corners and in front of the local liquor store, chatting up the neighborhood 'gangstas'.

"The changes in their make-up and dress signified the changes in their personality," Clark said. "They grew bored during their time at prep school. Even ashamed. They did not want to see themselves as nerds and hated that aspect of themselves. Starting in eighth grade, it was time to start rebelling. By the time they reached high-school, the thug life was part of their persona. Dark make-up. Tattoos. Hanging out with gang bangers. Alcohol and drugs. But most important, they wanted all the drama that came with that kind of life. Who is out to get who, who dissed who and who shot who became their modus operandi in life."

Grandfather Gilbert, however, had seen this all before as a Chicago cop. He feared that the girls, particularly Regina, would become ensnared by the street gang culture. He tried to obstruct this from happening and found Regina a job with a local periodontist. He figured if he kept the girl busy with school and work it would keep her away from the idiots on the street.

Regina, however, did not have the emotional maturity to see the light. She showed up late for her first couple of shifts then she was fired.

But she had started dating a man named Johnny Rivera, a known member of Chicago's notorious "Latin Kings" street gang. Rivera had a rap sheet as long as "War and Peace" as well as more aliases than a Russian spy

Regina would learn how to package and deal drugs at the foot of Johnny. She would watch him put the cocaine into plastic bags, measuring it out by the ounce. They would drive around town and Johnny would introduce her to his customers, watching as he conducted the deals. The secret handshakes and secret lingo all became apart of Regina's world.

Officially crossing over from innocent prep school girl to drug dealing girlfriend, Regina lived a double life. She did manage to get a part-time job doing data entry work for a local law firm and had enrolled in the local junior college (Harold Washington).

Margaret was getting into trouble as well. Her grades in high school were slipping as she would sneak out at night to be with friends. She would often come to school looking "disheveled" according to one teacher who thought she looked like a child whose parents were going through a divorce.

And there was trouble on the home front.

Neighbors would report hearing the girls fighting with their mother on a daily basis.. The two girls were out of control with no father figure to put them in line. Nora would berate Regina whenever she would act up in school or get arrested and the girls would yell back.

In private, Nora would refer to her daughters as "the bitches".

Things would come to a head when Regina would get arrested for selling cocaine to an undercover cop. A single mom already strapped for cash as she had to support three children on her own, Nora was livid as she paid Regina's bail.

"How are you going to pay me back?" .

"I don't know!"

"Do you know how much it costs to bail you out of jail!" Nora screamed. "You are going to pay me back. You're going to pay me back every penny!"

CHAPTER TWO

"She needs money," Margaret said, her voice full of concern.

"How much?" Oscar asked.

"One thousand dollars. Can you help us out, baby?"

That was the scene set for the twenty-two year old Oscar Velazquez in June of 2000 as he spoke to the sister of his current teenage crush, Regina DeFrancisco. He spotted Regina around the neighborhood of Pilsen and quickly fell for her dark Irish-Italian good looks. Showing off his brand new Z28 Camaro, he chatted up the girls before he asked Regina out for tacos. The two began going out but Regina didn't like him...at first. Then she realized that he had some money and was all too willing to spend it on her.

"Oscar wasn't the typical guy that Regina would go for," Clark said. "Regina liked the 'bad boy', the thug. Oscar wasn't in street gang culture. He had immigrated from Mexico and actually had a real job, earning his living the old fashioned way as a truck driver. If anything, Regina would see someone like him as a sucker, someone who she could use."

Still, Regina was what Oscar wanted. He persisted in calling her, asking when he could see her again.

"He's a creepy guy," Regina told her sister, Margaret as her cell phone rang. She looked at the caller ID. Yep, it was Oscar.

"But maybe you can get some money from him?"

"Here, you talk to him," Regina said handing the cell phone to Margaret. "Just make up some baloney that I'm in jail or something."

"What?"

"Get rid of him. Tell him I need bail money."

"Hello, Oscar?" Margaret answered the phone.

wanted to be 'gangstas', they wanted to be seen as 'hard'. They didn't have the maturity or the experience to realize that all of those 'gangstas' that they look up to are in jail. They didn't see Oscar at all. He was less than human. Something that is used, discarded and desecrated when it is no longer of use."

CHAPTER FOUR

Oscar was surprised that Regina finally called him back.

"Hey," she said, her teenaged voice soft and inviting.

"You're out of jail?" he asked.

"Yeah," she said. "I really appreciate what you did for me. That was really sweet of you."

"No worries," he said. "I need my money back. Been calling you like crazy."

"I'm sorry, I've just been busy."

"Yeah, I understand. But I need my money back."

"I was wondering if there was some other way I can pay you back?" she said in a sensual tone of voice.

"Like?"

"Like, I know you think my sister is hot, right?"

"What's that got to do with anything?"

"It is something we've been thinking about," she said. "But if you're not cool with it, it's okay."

"Not cool with what?"

"We were wondering if," Regina giggled. "If you can come over for a threesome."

Oscar couldn't believe his luck. He had heard of white girls being freaky, he just didn't think he would ever be able to experience it himself.

Naive to their plan, he rushed over and parked his car outside their mother's home in the South Side of Chicago.

He knocked on the door and was greeted by Margaret and Veronica Garcia, a friend of the two sisters. He didn't see the .38 caliber semi-automatic pistol had in her back waistband.

"Does anyone else know you're coming over?" Margaret asked.

"No," Oscar mumbled, shrugging his shoulder.

Margaret nodded her head and let the young man in. He saw Regina step into the room holding a bin of dirty laundry.

An awkward silence ensued followed by even more awkward smiles. The two sisters fed off each others willingness to go through with the plan. Even if one of them had second thoughts, they would be deemed "soft" by the other.

They had to go through with the murder.

Both women looked over at the young man with come hither looks. Regina said nothing as she opened the basement door and walked down.

"You go with Regina," Margaret said smiling.

"Right," Oscar said, his heart pounding in anticipation as he followed her down.

Oscar heard Margaret's footsteps behind him. What he didn't know was that she had a gun pointed at the back of his head.

When he reached the bottom step, she pulled the trigger.

The young man died instantly, falling face first in the tarp.

"Holy shit!" Margaret said. "I had no idea it would be that fucking loud. It doesn't sound that loud on TV."

Margaret came down the stairs. She kicked Oscar in the head hard, sending more blood spraying across the floor and wall.

"Nobody heard," Regina said as she knelt down and began rifling through Oscar's pockets.

"What the fuck was that?" Veronica said, calling down from the top of the basement steps.

"Did you see that? " Margaret asked. "He fell down like a baby!"

The sisters took out his wallet which had over $600 cash. They took his cell phone then ripped off the sterling silver chain from his neck.

"What the fuck happened?" Veronica said, her voice trembling as she came down a few steps.

"We shot his ass," Margaret said. "He's dead. Look at that shit, he's bleeding through his ears."

"Why did you do it?" Veronica screamed. "Why? Oh my God!"

"Shut the fuck up!" Margaret screamed.

"Don't just stand there," Regina commanded. "Come and help."

Their lifelong friend could only watch as the two sisters took out his car keys and wrapped up his body in a flowery bed sheet.

CHAPTER FIVE

"The girls suffered from what I call the 'Lord of the Flies' syndrome," Clark said. "Here they are hanging out with drug dealers, obtaining guns, killing men in the basement. There is no parental figure in sight! They are left to fend for themselves and the end result is murder and mayhem."

With the dead body in the basement, both sisters peeked out their window, waiting for dark.

Confident that the entire neighborhood was asleep, they opened the door and carried Oscar's body out of the home.

The three girls struggled carrying the dead weight, wrapping his body with a comforter and the flowered bed sheet.

They opened up the trunk and placed the body inside.

"What are you guys doing?" a woman yelled from a window across the street.

The girls looked up startled.

"We're getting rid of some furniture" Regina called out. "No worries."

The girls waved at the neighbor as she moved away from the window.

"Nosy bitch," Regina whispered.

Margaret giggled. Veronica still scared, said nothing.

They got into the vehicle and drove to a vacant lot where they took out Oscar's body again.

"This is hard work," Regina complained. "Shit!"

They plopped the body on the ground, looking at it for a beat before Regina reached back into the trunk. She pulled out a bottle of nail polish remover and poured the liquid over the tarp.

"Are you sure that's gonna work?" Margaret asked.

"It says 'highly flammable,'" Regina said, shrugging her shoulders.

Margaret lit a match and set the material on fire.

The flame went up immediately, the girls could feel the warmth on their faces in the cold Chicago night.

"Told you this shit would work!" Regina said.

Then as fast as the flame started, it quickly died down.

"Light another one," Regina said.

Margaret threw down another match, getting the flames going again as Regina doused the tarp with the remaining nail polish remover.

Satisfied, the girls quickly got back into the Camaro and drove off.

**

An anonymous call came into police headquarters reporting the fire in the vacant lot. The caller investigated further, however, and saw Oscar's arm sticking out through the fire. He called 911 again with a sense of urgency, telling them of the body.

CHAPTER SIX

When police on scene identified Oscar Velazquez' partially burned body, their initial knee-jerk reaction was that this was the work of a local street gang, a drug deal gone awry. But when they found the nail polish remover bottle, however, they quickly realized that this was the work of amateurs. A jealous girlfriend maybe.

Meanwhile, the DeFrancisco sisters cruised around town over the following days, trying to pawn off the Camaro.

"This is where the sisters make the guys in 'Dumb and Dumber' look like geniuses," Clark said. "They had only pre-planned the front end of the murder. Like most impulsive killers, they had no idea what to do after. Their greed took over and they decide to sell the Camaro. They have no papers for it, duh, and really can only sell a stolen vehicle to a thug. They find no takers as even the dumbest street gang member isn't going to buy a hot car from two teenaged girls. So they cruise around town and Oscar's brother spots them in the car."

The girls, failing in their sales efforts, would later abandon he vehicle behind a storefront and set it on fire.

**

The day after Oscar's killing, a mutual friend named Jessica Benitez stopped by the house. Jessica went downstairs and watched Margaret mop up a stain of blood near the basement steps.

"The hell is that?" she asked.

Margaret said nothing as she poured bleach over the blood, scrubbing hard.

"Dude bled all over the floor," Regina said. "But only after Margaret kicked him in the head. We called him over, told this idiot we'd have a threesome with him. Then we robbed his ass."

"But the blood stain on the floor-" Jessica asked, watching Margaret clean up.

"We killed a guy," Margaret said without remorse.

"He was going to kill us!" Regina said. "Margaret shot him in the back of the head. We searched his body and found a gun in his waistband. Then we wrapped him up in plastic and put him in his car."

"Holy shit, girl," Jessica.

"We're about to go on the run," Margaret announced.

"Aren't you scared?" Jessica asked, looking back down at the blood stain in the basement.

"I ain't scared of nothing," Margaret said. "You should have seen his head when I shot him. His brain oozed out like cheese."

Margaret made a rolling motion with her hands.

Jessica then accompanied Margaret to the store she purchased a bottle of blonde hair dye for her "disguise."

"We see here how the whole street gang culture has influenced the behavior of these girls," Clark said. "At any point in time, Veronica or Jessica could have went straight to the police. But they get caught up in the drama of the moment. The so-called 'loyalty' to their friend who, quite frankly, would shoot them up in a heartbeat if they knew that they were going to be a snitch."

Going off the tip from Oscar's brother, the police show up to question both Regina and Margaret. The duo denied ever seeing Oscar.

They then go to interview Veronica Garcia.

They found the jittery fifteen year old to be a different story, however. The teen quickly crumbled under the pressure of questioning and told the police the entire story.

Feeling the heat, the DeFrancisco sisters go on the run...

CHAPTER SEVEN

For all of their stupidity in committing the murder, the DeFrancisco sisters deftly avoided capture for almost two years.

They decided to split up. Margaret would go to live with their maternal aunt in Roscoe, Illinois, an hour and a half drive away from where they lived. Roscoe was a small town with less then 10,000 people, a far cry from the drug infested streets of Chicago. Margaret's worst dreams were now realized. She was now a nerd who had to stay inside all day long, living in a boring cul-de-sac with no street gang action. Neighbors would remark that they would never see her and if hey did she would quickly go back inside.

Living underground without detection, it took a broadcast of the television show AMERICA'S MOST WANTED to generate an anonymous tip which led to Margaret's whereabouts. Police staked out her aunt's apartment and entered, finding Margaret in her bedroom with a blank look on her face.

"My feelings were hurt bad because she (my wife) did something behind my back," Margaret's uncle by marriage said later. "I knew (police) were going to find her anyway."

Seven months later, Regina was captured in Dallas living with her Latin King boyfriend, Johnny Rivera.

Initially, she did not even know where the gang banger lived. She just knew the town, Laredo, and she journeyed there by bus. Regina would eventually find him, locating one of his relatives. She would live under an alias and claimed that she worked as a maid.

Police knew better. Regina made money by selling drugs under the Latin King banner.

Unlike Margaret, Regina had evaded the scrutiny of the America's Most Wanted viewers.

Her capture came about because she could not stop hanging out with the wrong crowd.

Two sheriffs were had mistakenly arrived at her boyfriend's apartment, wanting to serve a warrant to someone else.

Rivera allowed the deputies to enter his apartment but he had left a marijuana flake on his table. Police searched the apartment further and found several packages of crack cocaine ready to be sold.

The deputies arrested Rivera. They searched inside the apartment and interviewed Regina, who was groggy from a cocaine high. She showed them her false Texas identification and they let her go.

But the deputies smelled something fishy on her aside from marijuana. They had the apartment manager set up a meeting with her. She arrived at the complex in an SUV with another man. The police approached and the SUV sped away.

The high-speed chase down residential Dallas streets reached upwards of 90 mph. The SUV then slammed into a center median, the front tires blowing out.

Regina got out of the car and tried to sprint away. A deputy tackled her and they fell to the ground, her cell phone skidding across the gravel road. Sifting through her pockets, the officer found over $1,500 cash.

She was taken to Dallas County Jail where they discovered her true identity.

"We pulled her out of jail," said a Deputy Dodson. "I asked to see one of her tattoos, and she showed me...I called her by name, but she never said a word to me. She knew it was over."

She was then extradited to Illinois to stand trial for the murder of Oscar Velazquez.

CHAPTER EIGHT

The trial of the two women began in July of 2004 and both sisters pleaded not guilty by reason of self-defense.

But their friend, Veronica Garcia, had cut a deal with prosecutors in return for a lesser sentence. She would provide the testimony that would damn the two sisters to prison.

Garcia said that she didn't know what the sisters had planned. She had simply provided the gun to the DeFrancisco's which she thought would be used for a robbery only.

"I didn't see her shoot Oscar," Veronica said.

The prosecution brought forth additional witnesses in Jessica Benitez, Luciana Macias, and Maria Constantino, the neighbor.

"Both of them told me that they killed Oscar," Jessica said. "Margaret kicked him in the head so he could die faster."

"I saw them load the body into the back of the Camaro," Constantino said. "Regina told me that she planned out the killing."

Margaret, however, maintained their innocence. She said that Oscar came to the apartment angry because the sisters had tricked him out of one-thousand dollars.

"I shot him to protect Regina," Margaret said.

"Then why didn't you tell the reporting officer what happened?" the prosecution attorney asked.

"We would've got in trouble," Margaret said. "If I told the truth, I would've been there longer."

Regina DeFrancisco would also take the stand and claim self-defense as well.

"I came out of my bedroom," Regina said. "And he was there, cursing and screaming. He pulled a gun on me. I thought I was going to die. I curled up on the floor, in a fetal position. I begged for my life. Then I heard a gunshot and saw Margaret standing over Oscar, holding a gun."

"Whose idea was it to dispose of the body?"

"Veronica knew of this vacant lot," Regina said. "It was her idea."

The jury would deliberate for over six and a half hours. Regina would be found guilty of murder. Margaret's jury, however, was unable to convict her. There was and 11 to 1 deadlock with one juror believing that she should be acquitted. The juror did not believe that someone so young could commit murder.

Margaret was then released from custody and told to await retrial. She had a baby during this time, a girl, and would find work as a nursing assistant while she awaited another trial.

Four months later, Margaret would be given another day in court. Veronica Garcia would once again be the star witness for the prosecution, detailing the exact same testimony as before.

There would be no deadlock in this second go around as Margaret would be convicted of first-degree murder.

Regina would be sentenced to 35 years in prison while Margaret would be sentenced to 46 years. Both women are now jailed at the Dwight Correctional Center. They have each filed appeals which have been denied.

"The girls cared nothing about Oscar Velazquez," Clark said. "In the end, they remained true to their own narcissistic nature. They only cared about what was happening to the next. They cared about nothing about the now fatherless children Oscar Velazquez would leave behind nor about the fact that the took his life."

Veronica Garcia was jailed for five years. She served her full sentence and has since been released.

"This is a cautionary tale if there ever was one," Clark said. "The sisters had it all. They had access to one of the finest schools in their state. Yet they chose to throw it all away for short money and the cheap thrill of the 'thug life.' In the end, they got to see what the 'thug life' was really all about. Mindless violence where everyone is out for themselves, especially when there is a plea bargain to be made. They could have had it all had they stayed on the straight and narrow. Now they have nothing."

KILLER NURSE BEVERLY ALLITT

33

JENNIFER PARRIS

Beverly Allitt-the Angel of Death

It is hard to believe that a young female could be capable of murder, let alone multiple murders. It is even more shocking that a female nurse could carry out such terrible crimes. That is exactly what Beverly Allitt did though. This nurse is Britain's most infamous female serial killer and also goes by the name of the Angel of Death due to her responsibility to care for others but instead used her nursing position to kill people. Over a short period of fifty-nine days in her job as a nurse in a children's ward, she killed four young children and attempted to kill at least nine others either by causing cardiac arrest or hypoglycemia. The Angel of Death did not appear to be an evil killer though. She was very well mannered with parents, which is how she gained their trust with their precious loved ones. But after similar/suspicious causes of death in the children's ward, investigations at the hospital showed missing nursing records and the presence of Allitt with every one of those cases.

Childhood

As a child, Beverly Allitt liked attention and would go about negative ways of getting it. She was born in October of 1968 and was one of four children (two sisters and one brother). Her father worked in an off-licence (a British shop where the liquor is sold off premises) and her mother cleaned schools. Neighbors described Allitt as affectionate because she liked to volunteer and often would babysit. She did her chores at home and saved the money she earned. Teachers also really liked her and was considered one of their favorites. She went to school at Charles Read Secondary Modern School because she failed the exam needed to attend Kesteven and Grantham Girls' School.

She often would wear casts and bandages as a kid without letting her injuries be examined. She got worse as she got older and became overweight. During this time in her life, she was sick and injured more frequently. She often engaged in self-injury and spent a lot of time in and out of various hospitals due to different ailments such as gall bladder pain, back trouble, ulcers, headaches, and blurred vision, just to name a few. Her reasons were that she had been hit on her bike by a passing car or had fallen off a horse or even had been burned. Most of her problems were either made up or self-inflicted. She convinced a doctor to take out her healthy appendix. Then, she constantly interfered with the scar to keep it from healing. Another time, she stabbed herself in the hospital with the intention of injecting her body with water. Next, there was the time when she tampered with a thermometer in the hospital. Because she was physically healthy, she had to see lots of different doctors in order to keep them treating her.

Allitt was a frequent liar and not just about her illnesses. She would often make up stories. One time, she told people that her parents had split up and that she would have to go live with her aunt. The tales would be investigated and found out to not be true.

Beverly Allitt dreamed of becoming a nurse and attended school at Grantham College and began her studies at the age of sixteen. During her last year of school, she was absent approximately one hundred and twenty-six days with numerous illnesses. Nurses there also described her as odd. There were some at the school that thought Allitt would benefit from psychiatric help.

She did manage to find a boyfriend at Grantham College really only because she forced Stephen Biggs to be hers. He bought her a ring but she never set a date for the wedding and refused to hold his hand in public. Once, she faked a pregnancy. She said that Stephen had AIDS. Another time, she lied about being raped by a former boyfriend. Allitt was described as deceptive by her boyfriend.

Eventually, Allitt's odd injuries (real or fake) were thought to be from a controversial personality disorder known as Munchausen Syndrome. People with this disorder like to be ill because of the attention they get from others when they are sick as well as the satisfaction of fooling doctors with their self-inflicted illnesses and injuries. They often have long medical histories. They are frequent liars and have lab tests that lead to no answers for the doctors to diagnose a patient. Allitt may have liked the attention because even though her childhood seemed to be relatively normal, there could have been emotional needs that were not being met.

Nursing Career

Beverly Allitt went on to become a nurse but the odd behavior from her childhood still continued. She took her nursing exams and actually failed them because she was absent quite often due to her various illnesses.

After that, Allitt managed to find a job at a nursing home. Like at school, she was gone quite often. Once, when she was there, it was thought that she smeared feces on the walls.

In 1991, at the age of twenty-three, Beverly Allitt surprisingly got a six-month contract job at Grantham and Kesteven Hospital that is located in Lincolnshire working in the children's ward. This ward was for newborn babies up to the age of sixteen. Kids sent to this hospital often had minor illnesses. They were quickly treated and then sent home as soon as they were well.

When Allitt arrived at the hospital, she had had less than two years of experience at this point and was not even a qualified children's nurse. It was shocking that she even was considered for a job considering how many days of class she missed when attending nursing school. The only reason she got the job was because the hospital was understaffed and no one else applied for the job. At the time, there were only two day nurses and one night nurse. According to one of those nurses, Mary Reet, who worked at the hospital at the same time as Allitt, "There was something about her that I didn't like but couldn't pinpoint it" (Birmingham Mail). She thought that she seemed cheerful, friendly, and helpful, however. Allitt was even respected. She was the one calling the alarms and identifying problems that the very sick children were experiencing.

Because of her job working with others, it meant that she was no longer getting personal attention but it allowed her to find attention in other ways that were just as negative as when she was a kid. The nurse was able to use this opportunity to get close to the patients. Allitt was able to befriend all of her patients' parents by suggesting that they leave to go get some coffee. Through this recommendation, the parents were trusting her and allowing her to be alone to administer treatment to the children. The parents had really appreciated the nurse at the time because of her actions during this difficult time when their children were sick. It was her care and love for her patients that caused the parents to call her an angel. She would even ride with the patients in the ambulance if they needed to be transferred to another hospital. However, Allitt was far from an angel. The term *Angel of Death* is given to medical professionals that are supposed to be healing patients but are really causing them harm.

The angel changed a week after she arrived at the hospital and odd things began to happen. Money was being stolen from the nurses.

A key to the insulin refrigerator had disappeared. This is also when the young patients began experiencing odd symptoms that were very serious. Some of the patients died. At Grantham and Kesteven Hospital, usually only one child died a year. Once Allitt started working, four children died in just a period of a few months.

The Victims

Allitt's reign of terror began on February 21, 1991. Though it is not exactly clear how many children she actually did harm, the definite numbers are four murders and nine that were purposely harmed all within a fifty-nine-day time period. The ages of her patients were between seventeen weeks to eleven years old.

Seven-month-old Liam Taylor was Beverly Allitt's first victim. He had a chest infection and had come to the hospital for treatment. Since Allitt was able to befriend the parents, they left the hospital to get some rest. Once they returned, they learned from her that Liam had experienced respiratory problems but had recovered. She tried to convince the parents to leave again but they chose to stay. He suffered more respiratory problems under Allitt. She let the emergency team at the hospital know once he started becoming pale. The other nurses on the floor were confused because no alarms sounded when he had stopped breathing. He did survive but he had suffered cardiac arrest and brain damage. He was put on life support and was later taken off of it by his parents. His death at the time was ruled as heart failure.

Timothy Hardwick was Allitt's next victim. He was the oldest victim at eleven. He had cerebral palsy and dealt with seizures. The emergency team was notified when the boy turned blue and had no pulse. Allitt stood by as the defibrillator was used. Unfortunately, the boy died. There was an autopsy performed but there were no answers to the cause of his death. Epilepsy was eventually ruled as the cause.

The third victim was one-year-old Kayley Desmond. She had a chest infection but was getting better. After being in the care of Allitt though, she went into cardiac arrest. She was revived and transferred to another hospital. Once there, doctors discovered that there was a puncture hole under her armpit and also an air bubble. It was decided that it was probably due to an accidental injection. Because Kayley was transferred to the other hospital, she did survive.

Allitt's next victim was five-month-old Paul Crampton. He had been admitted for a minor infection. The nurse was not actually on duty when he was admitted but after she took over, Paul's condition deteriorated. He experienced an episode of insulin shock and nearly went into a coma. The Angel of Death was the one that raised the alarm about his serious condition. Doctors were very confused about the changes in insulin levels. After a few days, Paul began to feel better and Allitt was asked by the doctor to remove his drip. Shortly after that, he became quite ill for the second time. When he started feeling better, the dad decided to take a short break from the hospital room. The nurse was once again left in charge and the baby suffered the third attack. He was transferred to another hospital. Allitt actually went with him in the ambulance. She was also the one that had suggested that the doctors test the baby's blood sugar. Thankfully, Paul survived at the other hospital. After a few weeks, his test results came back. He had actually had 43,147 milliunits of insulin in his blood. That is one of the highest levels found in a human. The only other person that had levels this high died. It was a wonder that Paul survived with Allitt as his nurse.

Next on Allitt's list was Bradley Gibson at five years old. He had pneumonia and under the care of the Angel of Death, went into cardiac arrest. It was discovered that he also had high insulin. That night, he had a heart attack but was transferred to a second hospital and was able to survive.

Yik Hung Chan was two when he came to the hospital to recover from a fractured skull from a fall. He ended up turning blue while Allitt was working. He was given oxygen, transferred to another hospital, and recovered. The nurse was not blamed though because it was thought that the fracture was behind the boy's symptoms.

Next, Beverly focused her attention on twins on two different occasions. The twins were born premature and were under her supervision. The first twin, Becky, was found to have been cold and hypoglycemic but was released that evening. Then, that night, Becky woke up in pain but a doctor just said it was colic. She died that night. That is why the second twin, Katie, came back to the hospital for observation. Katie stopped breathing a couple of times while there. Her lungs collapsed and she suffered from brain damage and was transferred to another hospital. There, it was also discovered that five of her ribs had been broken but surprisingly, she lived. Her parents were so happy that they asked Allitt to be Katie's godmother. She agreed despite Katie having to live with partial paralysis, sight and hearing damage, and cerebral palsy.

After this, there were four additional victims that also suffered from similar symptoms as the other patients over a short period of fifteen days. There was seven-year-old Michael Davidson, nine-month-old Christopher King, eight-month-old Christopher Peasgood, and seven-week-old Patrick Elstone. Patrick was oxygen deprived and became brain damaged. People were starting to get suspicious about what was going on at this hospital.

Finally, Claire Peck, age fifteen months, became Allitt's last victim. This little baby had asthma and required a breathing tube. She was only under the care of the nurse for a couple of minutes when she had a heart attack. She survived but then had a second one later, leading to her death. It was thought that her death was because of natural causes. It was later found that she had been injected with lignocaine. This drug is not administered to babies. Claire was the Angel of Death's last victim after fifty-nine days of work.

The Investigation

After the numerous number of cardiac cases in the last few months at Grantham and Kesteven Hospital, an inquiry was launched into the cause of all of them. Deaths and comas at children's hospitals are actually pretty rare; especially if they are unexplained. At this particular children's hospital, usually only one child died a year. At first, it was thought that maybe there was a virus in the air that was making the patients sicker than when they arrived. This turned out to be incorrect. The nurses on the floor, including Beverly Allitt, talked about how maybe there was a parent or some outsider sneaking in and causing harm. That was when security cameras were placed in the hospital and the staff became more careful. They were also being watched by other people that worked in the hospital.

Next, it was discovered that there was a lot of potassium in Claire's blood. The police were called into the investigation and realized that there was lignocaine in Claire's system. This drug is given to people during cardiac arrest but is never given to a baby.

It was then that the police began to suspect that all the deaths were probably not due to natural causes. In fact, there were a lot of victims that had had high levels of insulin. To figure out what was going on, the police had a secret meeting with the hospital management to talk about a possible killer. After that, information came about that Allitt had actually reported that the key to the refrigerator where the insulin was stored had gone missing.

The next thing to do was check the daily nursing logs. Coincidentally, they were missing. The pages for the time of Paul Crampton's visit had been torn out of the book. There was also another record book that was gone. The pages were actually discovered at Allitt's house. The missing records along with her presence at every incident involving the mysteriously ill children led to her arrest.

Mary Reet, one of Allitt's coworkers was actually stunned at first to hear of her arrest. She was sure that the police had made a mistake. In fact, Katie's parents wanted to protect their daughter's godmother.

They hired a detective to help prove her innocence. They even let the nurse continue to babysit Katie. Other people in the United Kingdom were also shocked. There had never been a nurse that had killed patients in the country. But with the evidence that had been collected, there was definitely no mistake about who was guilty of harming thirteen or more innocent hospital patients that were all so very young.

The Arrest/Trial

The police thought that they had enough evidence to convict Allitt but she was not actually charged until several months later. When interrogated, she did not seem scared about talking to the police. She denied any wrongdoing and said that all she had been doing was caring for the ill children. She even claimed that she was not at the hospital on some of the days in question and that at the other times she had come on the scene later and that she had been trying to help like a good nurse would do. At that point, the police did not have enough evidence to convict her so they had to let her go for the time being but that still did not erase their suspicions and she was suspended from the hospital. After all, the events at the hospital were certainly suspicious. Also, the other nurses said that she never liked to pick up crying babies and that she never seemed saddened by the deaths of any of the children. Later, she was eventually arrested.

With the investigation of Allitt's Munchausen Syndrome that led her to desire attention through the suffering of various medical conditions, it was also found that she dealt with Munchausen Syndrome by Proxy. This personality disorder is very similar to Munchausen Syndrome but instead of making oneself ill, the individual makes another one ill in order to get attention. People with Munchausen Syndrome sometimes also have Munchausen Syndrome by Proxy like Allitt. In Beverly situation, when the nurse found that she was no longer getting attention for her own medical disorders, she switched to causing them because she was able to receive attention from parents and other nurses by acting like the hero for the victims when she cared for them. The victims of people with Munchausen Syndrome by Proxy are usually children because they are unable to speak up for themselves. Allitt was made out to look like a hero at times while still working at the hospital because she was caring for the children that had become seriously ill. She was even able to diagnose some of the children's ailments rather than the doctors since she had caused the illnesses. Such as in the case of Katie, the twin, Allitt was made godmother which gave her the attention she craved.

Despite her love of attention, she did not want the attention for being a criminal. She wanted what she thought was positive attention in which people pitied her since she was sick quite often.

Allitt was evaluated by medical professionals for her disorders while in jail but she never did confess to the crimes. While she was awaiting trial however, Allitt lost a ton of weight which developed into anorexia. This was just another example of the psychological problems she experienced. Because of all of her past (and now present) illnesses, she repeated her absenteeism from nursing school and only attended sixteen days of the two-month long trial.

The trial was difficult because even though the evidence pointed to her, there were no fingerprints or any eyewitnesses. Everything was circumstantial. It had taken nearly nine months to gather the evidence that had been presented in court. The police were definitely worried about what the jury would decide. The jury deliberated for six days before they made the big decision about the Angel of Death.

She was eventually charged with four counts of murder, eleven counts of attempted murder, as well as eleven counts of causing serious harm to her patients. The parents of the victims, including the police, were overjoyed with the verdict. Justice would be served for what she had done to their children. The nurse was then given thirteen life sentences in 1993 for the murder and attempted murder of the innocent children that became her victims. Munchausen Syndrome by Proxy had no impact on the judge's decision of the extremely severe sentence that was given to Allitt. This is actually the harshest punishment ever given to a female. The judge said that he recommended that she spend at least forty years in prison before parole would even be considered but it became thirty years. As the judge said when she was sentenced, "You have turned the hospital where you worked into a killing field" (Birmingham Mail).

Allitt will be 54 in 2022 when the thirty-year possible parole could even become a possibility. It will only happen though if she has become a reformed person and is no longer a danger to herself or to anyone else. It does not change that she is still a murderer, despite having the label of Munchausen Syndrome or Munchausen Syndrome by Proxy. Though it does not seem likely that she will be released, the parents of the victims say that no matter what, they will fight back if there ever comes a chance of her leaving the prison/hospital where she is serving her time.

Prison

Allitt was sent to Rampton Secure Hospital in Nottingham to serve her sentence under the Mental Health Act. This hospital is a facility that has high security to protect prisoners suffering from mental disorders. It is not a prison because the patients/prisoners are there to receive treatment. Chris Taylor, the father of Liam Taylor, was not pleased with her placement. He thought she should be sent to jail and that it would not matter whether she killed herself in prison or not. She was sent to the hospital by the judge because of her history of self-harm. Taylor, however, looks at it as a place to take a vacation because she has a TV and is allowed to talk to other people at the hospital to form relationships with them. There is a bar and the hospital throws discos. Occasionally, Allitt has even been allowed to go out shopping as long as she is with a guard. During an interview, the former nurse mentioned that she liked the place because of the freedom it gave her that she would not receive in jail. In order for prisoners like Beverly Allitt to enjoy the freedom while receiving treatment, it costs the taxpayers of the United Kingdom £2000 a week for each inmate to stay there.2000

Her problems with Munchausen Syndrome have not ended despite being at Rampton Secure Hospital in order to receive her treatment. Once she arrived, she ate glass, stabbed herself with paperclips, and poured boiling water on her hands. On the plus side, she did admit to three of the murders and to six of the attempted ones.

Beverley was a young nurse that should have had the desire to help young children and be an advocate and a voice for them in order to heal. Growing up, she craved attention and went about negative ways to get it. She would either purposely hurt herself or lie about being ill in order to get attention. Things did not get better as she got older. Instead, she took advantage of her position at the hospital where she worked as a children's nurse. She harmed and killed many children so that she could get attention for herself. Through her attention desiring ways, she killed four children and hurt at least eleven more in the fifty-nine days that she worked as a children's nurse. Parents trusted the woman that later would become known as the Angel of Death. She will no longer be able to hurt another patient or child anymore since she has been given thirteen life sentences and will unable to be eligible for parole for at least thirty years (and that is only if she is able to show that she is no longer a danger to society).

GWEN HENDRICKS

DORA ENGLISH

Gwen Gillespie Hendricks was born into a Navy family in Memphis, Tennessee in 1955.

Her father was a naval officer while her mother was a housewife. Like most military families, they moved often from station to station, according to her father's assignment. Growing up in a devoutly Catholic home and Gwen would embrace the religion with fervor.

Gwen dressed with modesty, wearing button down shirts and minimal make-up. She fostered a nerd look, with wire-rimmed glasses and short hair.

Carrying on the family's military tradition, she joined the Air Force at the age of twenty-five. It was there she would meet Jim Hendricks, twenty-four, who was her instructor.

Jim Hendricks was a tall, strapping Air Force sergeant with an air of authority. He had an easy smile and Gwen found him easy on the eyes.

"Well, it was kind of instant attraction," Gwen recalled. "There was a bit of lust there as he's a very tall, handsome man. The Air Force can tell you that you can't date but they can't tell you who to marry so I went to the Jag office and asked if I could marry my STA and they said 'yes.'"

The two were married in 1980. Jim had a five year old daughter, Season Hendricks, from a previous relationship. In 1982, they would have a son, Ben.

Because of their career choice, the couple spent a lot of time apart during the early years of their marriage. Jim was stationed at Wake Island while Gwen was assigned to Eglin Air Force Base in Florida.

The couple would be reunited in 1986 as Jim was assigned to the Air Force Academy in Colorado Springs. Gwen would not re-enlist in the Air Force, instead taking a job with the Internal Revenue Service.

The couple spent three years in Colorado before Jim would be transferred to Guam in August of 1989. He took the the entire family with him to the island.

"I figured we had a pretty normal family," Season said. "Until we moved to Guam. Things started to change. She (Gwen) would pick fights. She was jealous of the time my Dad and I would spend together."

"She (Gwen) had a different life in mind for herself," forensic psychologist Joyce Smith said. "She was used to having her own money. So when they moved to Guam there was little to do and less money to do it with."

Gwen and the children moved back to the United States, returning to Colorado and leaving Jim in Guam.

She would buy a home in Littleton and once again start working for the IRS. She then joined the junior Chamber of Commerce where she met Terry Knaack and a woman named Rochelle.

"Rochelle was into tarot cards," Gwen said. "And Terry was into new age occultism. My religion, my faith was still very meaningful to me. I wanted to do Bible study with them to get them out of what I considered witchcraft. Rochelle said she wouldn't go to Bible study with me unless I did the cards with her and the same with Terry. So I think I opened up the door to hell. Right after I started, everything went wrong"

During this time, Gwen began to experience health issues. She suffered from dizzy spells and nausea.

Her personality shifted as well, changing from being even-tempered to easily agitated and manic. With her health and ability to focus effected, Gwen stepped down from her revenue collector position to tax examiner.

"Could the illness have played a part in her deciding to kill her husband?" Smith asked. "Maybe. But Gwen was really steeped into religion and sounded like she embraced some of the more fringe elements of Christianity. She truly believed that occultism was a form of witchcraft and that those things could do her harm. So when she suffered from her illness she erroneously attributed it to her dabbling in the occult. She was a woman who preferred supernatural explanations to rational thought."

Gwen also started to grow deeper into debt, buying expensive gifts for friends.

In the fall of 1990, Gwen hired Terry Knaack to help remodel the Littleton home. A few months later, Knaack moved into the couple's basement with the rationale being he would be able to help with the mortgage. With the husband away and a man in the home, Gwen began to fantasize about Terry and starting over with him.

"Terry would talk a lot about wanting to having a ranch for children with special needs," Gwen recalled. "And I started having delusions that he and I would start this ranch together for the children."

"She entered into a fantasy world," Smith said. "She began imagining a life with this other man, having delusions of grandeur of what they would do together. He became her willing accomplice in her dreams, since her own husband was absent because of military duty. So an alternate universe with Terry Knaack became her obsession. What probably started as harmless day dreams soon grew into something sinister."

"I also believe that Gwen had more than a little bit of a Messiah complex. She had this compulsion to save people and it manifested in doling out gifts and handouts to people who she felt were in need. She had this secret life and kept things from Jim who was away on military assignment. Those secrets involved getting into credit card debt."

By January of 1991, Gwen began telling friends that she was having premonitions of Jim dying in a plane crash.

"I had this really bad dream over and over again," Gwen recalled. "Where Jim had died in a plane crash. I was thinking, well after Jim died that I would marry Terry and we'd start this ranch but of course Terry didn't know anything about because it was all in my head."

Gwen then began hearing voices.

"They (the voices) wanted me to sacrifice what was most dear in my life," Gwen recalled. "I remember thinking that I have to answer these voices because this is coming from God. You know, I've got to sacrifice what I loved the most and that was Jim."

Gwen kept a journal where she logged the "premonitions" of her husband's death. She titled the journal "The Courage to Will and Persevere," She described the voices that she heard and believed that God had told her to kill Jim.

"She experienced what we call 'command hallucinations,'" said Smith. "These are sometimes coupled with someone's value system, in this case, it was Gwen's religion. Gwen believed that she should obey God and believed that the voices that she heard were, in fact, coming from God. So this could go bad real quick if those voices told her to do damage to someone."

"She was past the breaking point, a delusional schizophrenic that was not diagnosed. When she confided with friends it was probably with people who shared her same point of view, people who believed in visions, messages from God and premonitions. Gwen was a soft-spoken woman and even if someone thought she was crazy they would not think she would be capable of taking a gun and blowing someone's brains out. She didn't have that violent vibe."

But behind closed doors, Gwen would deal with problems or difficulties in a haphazard fashion. She would often open up the Bible and believed that whatever random verse she came upon was a direct message from God.

"I reread Psalm 90 quite a few times before a small voice said, 'Keep reading, keep reading.'" Gwen wrote in her journal. "After reading the first page of stanzas, I knew I would be protected from the car bombs, the knifings, the guns, the contracts and all the other evil I had seen connected with busting the pornographers and pimps. Those mafia guys play rough, but somehow they just won't be able to get me. Then I turned the page to continue reading. It felt like a giant fist had slammed into my heart. I literally could not breath [sic]. I burst into sobs and sunk to the floor. I cried for Jim because he really was going to die."

Gwen began to prepare for Jim's death, taking out a $300,000 life insurance policy on her husband payable on his death.

She then visited a local banker, informing him that she would be soon be receiving proceeds from insurance claim. Gwen was told that she would not be able to use the money as long as Jim was alive. She then forged a doctor's note which alleged that she had multiple sclerosis. She submitted this note to the Red Cross along with a letter stating that they should be responsible for being her husband back from Guam.

Gwen did not want the proceeds from the insurance for her own material gain. She believed that she could use the proceeds from his life insurance to establish the "James Hendricks Foundation" to aid victims of mafia produced pornography.

"She became obsessed with pornographers," Smith said. "Like most people with Messiah Complexes, she chose an ill of society and focused on that, believing that she was a chosen vessel to help eradicate the 'sin.' In her deluded mind, she needed this money to accommodate

God's will to establish this ranch wherein she would save victims of pornography. The only way she could attain this goal would be to kill Jim and take the life insurance proceeds."

"I was very desperate to have him (Jim) back," Gwen said. "I felt like I was at my limit and not really realizing that I actually was really having a breakdown."

With her husband not even dead yet, Gwen began purchasing clothes for herself and the children to wear for his funeral.

She bought silk flowers and boxes of Kleenex for mourning friends and family.

Gwen also increased the amount of Jim's life insurance from $300,000 to $1,000,000.

True to her premonition, she bought a wedding dress for herself and put a wedding ring on layaway for Knaack.

Gwen would ask God to speak to her directly and "guide her hand" as she thumbed through her Bible. When she got to a passage, she would believe that was what God wanted her to study."

"For the first reading, only the last sentence made sense," Gwen wrote. "I had asked if what I felt about Jim's death was real. He said yes.

God can even speak through the dictionary!

After reading the first page of stanzas, I knew I would be protected from car bombs, the knifings, the guns, the contracts and all the other evil I had seen connected with busting pornographers and pimps. Those Mafia guys play rough, but somehow they just won't be able to get me."

"You can see her delusions of grandeur in her journal writings," Smith said. "She had all of the symptoms of a delusional narcissist, truly believing that God made her as the 'Chosen One.'"

Gwen would write that she had a two-way conversation with God about creating the ranch.

"Oh, so the ranch is in Douglas county near to the Springs so my family will be protected from the mafia guys' Then I knew in Denver, I'm Gwen Hendricks. In the Springs, I'm Gwen Knaack. I had thought the clinic would carry the name of the ranch, but with this new insight, I knew that for safety sake, everything had to be kept separate."

She continued to have health issues as well, as the nausea and attacks of dizziness still had not subsided. Physicians could not determine the cause of her illness. She was eventually diagnosed with Ménière's disease, an ailment that causes vertigo and a fluctuating hearing loss. She had a micro-shunt placed into her ear which only helped relieve the pain she was experiencing.

Her mental health, however, continued to deteriorate.

Jim would return to Colorado for good in May of 1991. It would not be a well-received reunion, however, as the couple fought over everything specifically the living arrangements of Knaack. Jim promptly kicked the boarder out of the home.

He then took control of the finances as he discovered that Gwen had maxed out the credit cards.

"My brother said that she had apparently taken several other credit cards and had maxed them out to the limit," recalled Steve Hendricks, Jim's brother. "And he was furious with her at that point. He did confide in me that he was thinking about leaving Gwen."

Jim would take away all of Gwen's credit cards and this made her extremely angry.

"He took away her power," Smith said. "She got an ego boost by buying expensive gifts for friends and helping out women that she thought were in need. When Jim took that away, she saw him as someone who needed to be eliminated."

Divorce seemed imminent but Gwen seemed immune to it all in her journal writings.

"The funeral, the ranch school, children, the foundation, always being pushed forward," she wrote. "I have to do what I have to do, too. But just for now I'm going to take one day at a time. I'm hoping I don't get too compulsed to do anything more for at least this coming week. I need to rest.

Perhaps I should start by explaining the little voice. It's my voice, but not me. It comes from somewhere inside, and if I don't listen to it, act on it, it becomes a compulsion. If I don't listen and act on the compulsion, it grows stronger and stronger until it dominates all aspects of my life. I learned long ago to listen and do what I'm told. Things work out when I do, and when I don't, things get real miserable...Yes, my little voice is the way God reaches me with the Holy Spirit."

With Jim now home on a permanent basis, The voices in her head grew louder. They began to speak with more urgency in telling her that she had to kill her husband.

"True to her religious background, she did not interpret auditory hallucinations as a sign of mental illness," Smith said. "Gwen was the kind of woman who took the stories in the Bible literally, seeing herself as a modern day Abraham who heard voices from God. You hear it in the way she describes the voices in her head telling her to sacrifice her husband in the same way the Bible speaks of God telling Abraham to sacrifice his son Isaac."

"I said 'Lord I surrender to you,'" Gwen recalled. "I'm hearing voices from God and this is what God wants and I have to get this from God and if this is what God wants then I have to give it to him. So I went out and I bought a gun"

"The voices in her head told her it was time," Smith said. "And true to her value system, she had to obey. For her religion was not a therapeutic aid because of the way she had viewed it. Her God was a vengeful one, a violent one."

On Friday, August 17th, 1991 Gwen drove to Peterson Air Force Base to meet with her husband, a 75 mile drive, to bring him a change of clothes.

"Jim was working late and he asked me to bring him something to eat." Gwen said.

She had informed police that Jim was working all night to prepare for an inspection but changed his mind.

Gwen wrote in her journal about the incident.

When Jim called to say he was on his way home, I went into shock. I knew the time was at hand. I knew I wasn't really ready. I screamed and cried and raged. Then I asked again, if he was meant to die or was I just suckered into some kind of head game. Benjamin's daddy died. I cried myself to sleep that night. I thought what was I supposed to do with two husbands. God has the oddest sense of humor."

"She told me that she was gonna make a nice little picnic for them," Gwen's step-daughter Season recalled. "They were going to make a night of it and that she wanted him to feel good for his inspection."

Gwen left the home and dropped off both Season and son Ben with a friend. When Gwen arrived at the Air Force base, however, she stated that Jim told her that he was heading home. She maintained that the two then went back home in separate cars.

"His truck was in the lead," Gwen said. "I was in the car behind. I remember being so tired, I told him I can't go on anymore. I just want a quick nap and let's get in the back of the truck."

She said that they traveled in separate cars but she became tired and slept through the night at a rest stop along Interstate 25.

Police, however, believed that Gwen lured Jim to an abandoned stretch of highway with the promise of sex.

The two met at the side of the road and Gwen hesitated when thinking of pulling out the gun. She wanted her husband to go peacefully.

"I took the gun out from underneath the seat of the car," Gwen said. "I got into the truck and laid next to him and when I could feel that he was deeply sleeping that's when I shot him."

Gwen would shoot Jim six times.

"It was like I was outside of myself," Gwen said. "Looking and watching what I was doing. I felt very numb, very cold, like I was on auto-pilot. I got back into my car and I took apart the gun and I was just throwing the parts out the window and just driving around, just in a fog, not knowing what I was doing, where I was going. I stopped at a roadside rest stop. Fell asleep. When I woke up and I didn't know everything that happened."

When Gwen arrived back home that Saturday she began making calls to the police, stating that her husband was missing.

On Monday morning, she called Jim's supervisor who sent out two officers to search for him.

One of his co-workers would find his pickup truck on the side of Highway 83 in Douglas County. His body had been placed in the camper shell in back of his truck.

He had been shot six times in the chest and neck with a small caliber handgun.

Gwen would become the primary suspect.

Police noted that she hardly showed any emotion when they informed her of her husband's death.

"Her state of mind was that of a wife with a missing husband," one of the deputies recalled. "When she was telling a story, she couldn't stick with the same story. And that's a clue, obviously, to law enforcement."

Gwen would then break the news to Jim's daughter, Season.

"Gwen said they found him by the side of the road in his car," Season said. "And that he had been murdered. I don't remember her crying. It was the worst moment of my life."

Terry Knaack would be helpful in the case against Gwen. She had been secretly in love with him and given him her diary. He read through her writings and promptly delivered the diary to the Douglas County Sheriff's Department. The sheriffs then instructed him to call Gwen while they would listen in.

Gwen would tell Knaack that she didn't kill Jim but that she wanted to die. Then Douglas County Sheriff's Department Kim Castellano's intuition told her something was wrong. The Hendricks had two pre-teens, a boy and a girl and the boy was never around during questioning.

Castellano believed that Gwen had a problem with males. With one of the male investigators, an Air Force official, by her side, Castellano went back to talk to Gwen.

Once again, the boy was not there. Gwen was overly polite to Castellano, asking her if she wanted anything to eat and jumping up to fix her something before she could answer.

Gwen would totally ignored the male detective.

Castellano used this knowledge to her advantage and befriended Gwen, sensing that the delusional woman would be much more forthcoming with a female officer than a male.

Gwen began trusting her enough that she asked for Castellano's help in balancing her check book. The detective then saw that Hendricks had recently taken out several insurance policies that would be hers when her husband died.

The investigators then used a technique police refer to as the "midnight confession." Castellano and the Air Force official went over to the Hendricks house at eleven at night, waking Gwen up.

Questioning her in the family room, Gwen continued to deny her involvement in her husband's killing. Castellano and her partner then took turns reading from Gwen's journal, tightening the screws on her denial. They also saw Jim's watch on the counter.

Castellano then told her to get dressed and that she was being taken in.

Gwen finally cracked. She curled into a fetal position and confessed.

"Two stories that night—the story of the rest area and the story of Highway 83," she sobbed.

Gwen would go on to describe the highway story.

"There is blood everywhere, I can see it everywhere," she said. "It's terrible. My mind won't let me remember. I don't know if I shot him or not. I don't know what's real anymore."

Gwen was then taken to a local hospital where she stayed for two days for a mental health evaluation. She was arrested upon release and charged with her husband's murder.

After undergoing another mental health examination, Gwen was deemed delusional but understood the charges being levied against her.

Because of this, she was found fit to stand trial.

In court, however, Gwen continued to state that she didn't kill her husband. She said that the body found at the crime scene was not Jim's.

"There was the obvious choice for her attorneys to declare her insane," Smith said. "She had one hell of an imagination and could make things up on the fly. She said during the trial that she became completely convinced that her husband was still alive, going into full blown denial. 'He's still alive, he's out there somewhere and you have to find him', she would say. She was completely delusional."

Her first attorney, Lloyd Boyer, stated that it was physically impossible for Gwen to have murdered Jim Hendricks.

"The lack of gunshot residue inside the Capitol (Jim's car) vehicle," Boyer said. "Indicated that the murder had not occurred in the vehicle. Mr. Hendricks was quite a bit larger than Gwen and she was small, not especially strong and could not have moved the victim into the vehicle."

The investigators failed to produce the gun that Gwen used but the prosecution had another tool at its disposal.

The first link was Jim's watch that they found in Gwen's possession, which showed that she had tampered with the crime scene. The prosecution showed how she was going to use the money from the insurance policies and start a "home for troubled people" that would be near the spot where she killed her husband.

The jury found her guilty of first-degree murder and Hendricks was sentenced to life in prison.

"I just kept my faith that Jim would come rescue me and I would be set free from prison," Gwen said. "Of course, that never happened."

Inside the prison, physicians deemed her to be mentally unfit to be included with the general population and transferred her to the psychiatric unit.

"They got me on anti-psychotics," Gwen said. "And anti-depressants but it wasn't until 1997 that I started having memories of what had happened. At first, it was like just pictures and they hit me like bricks, you know. I killed a great husband and Dad. I robbed Season and Ben of their father. I felt lower than dirt."

She did have help, however, as some legal advocates filed briefs on her behalf, claiming that she had been insane at the time of her trial.

In September of 2000, the Supreme Court of Colorado overturned Gwen's conviction and ordered a new trial.

In April of 2001, a judge ruled that Gwen was not guilty by reason of insanity.

The trial lasted ten minutes.

"She came to terms with what she had done," Smith said. "She had stopped protesting, stop denying and admitted to what she had done."

Gwen was then remanded to a psychiatric care facility in Colorado. She then decided to change her name to "Emi Masai".

"When I lost Jim," Gwen said. "I also lost my children. I longed to be a wife and mother again. I redefined myself as married to Christ and being a mother to all the people I meet."

"By renaming herself she thought that she could obtain a new identity," Smith said. "It was a way of divorcing herself from her past transgressions."

Gwen went through four years of psychiatric treatment where the physicians determined that she was no longer a threat to society. She was released to a residential program where she now helps the needy at Mercy Ministries.

She continues to take her anti-psychotic medication.

"I never want to slip back into mental illness again," Gwen said. "I literally thank God every morning I open my medicine cabinet. I've always said justice wasn't done. Justice in this case would have been my execution. A life for a life. But it's not about fairness. It's about recognizing mental illness and knowing that you're not responsible for what you are doing when you're psychotic."

Gwen has had minimal contact with both her son and step-daughter since she committed the murder of their father.

"I long to see them but they let it be known through family channels that they don't want to see me," Gwen said. "So I respect that."

"I'm really glad that Gwen has helped herself enough to admit what she's done," Season said. "And I hope there never is a time where it gets easy for her to look in the mirror. Because there's never a time where it's easy to be without our Dad."

"I wish I could take it back," Gwen said. "Be a good wife and Mom again. I can't turn the clock back. So all I can do is give them my deepest apology and ask them to forgive me."

HOUSEWIFE, MOTHER & KILLER : THE TRUE STORY OF KIM HRICKO

62

DARLA PUGH

PROLOGUE

Kim Hricko was getting ready to kill her husband the night they attended a Valentine's Murder Mystery Party. Kim was a woman who was intelligent and determined, the irony of the play's theme was not lost on her.

It was destiny calling.

She watched with rapt attention as the actors went through the motions. A wedding bride took out a blue vial and poured the "poisonous" contents into her groom's champagne glass.

She has the right idea, Kim thought.

Looking over at her husband Steve, she imagined him in the place of the actor on stage, choking to death.

Could it be that easy?

CHAPTER ONE

"Kim Hricko was one of those people that you look at and say 'I would never have guessed,'" forensic psychologist Paula Orange said. "Something inside her snapped when she wanted out of her marriage. It could have been so simple. Call a lawyer and file for divorce. Kim wanted a lot more than that. She wanted blood."

Steve and Kim Hricko would be introduced by their mutual friends Maureen and Mike Miller at Penn State in 1984. Their temperaments seemed to be the perfect complement to one another, they would have a yin-yang compatibility.

"Kim was a very gregarious personality," Maureen said. "She was very outgoing. Very friendly. Everybody liked her."

"Steve was my best friend since seventh grade," Mike said. "Corny as it sounds we were kinda each others brother that we didn't have. My wife had set up a double date. He (Steve) was smitten by her. Thought she was very attractive. Basically, they hit it off and from that point on started dating."

Steve was a burly figure at 6'3" and 245 lbs. He was a star college football player but was on the shy side.

"He was a big teddy bear," Maureen said. "He just wanted everybody that he loved to be happy and for him to take care of them."

Neither Kim or Steve dated much before their union. Kim had a distant relationship with her father after her own parents divorced. Her mother would remarry a man that would sexually and physically abuse her.

Steve and Kim would marry and have a daughter. Nine years into their marriage, Steve would still be smitten by the woman that the Millers had set him up with. Kim, however, would have feelings of resentment that built up over time.

Temperamentally, the couple did not match up well. Steve was an introvert. Kim an extrovert. Kim hung out with doctors and nurses while Steve just wanted to stay home. He didn't feel welcome into Kim's elite social circle, put off by their large houses and flashy cars.

But Steve remained in love with Kim despite that over the years she did not treat him with the same warmth as she once did. She was now cold and disinterested toward her spouse.

Steve blamed himself for the deterioration and began working to save his marriage.

His efforts would only serve to pour fuel on the fire...

CHAPTER TWO

Kim fed up with the loveless relationship, suggested that they get a divorce but Steve refused. He also dismissed the idea of counseling but after nine years he finally saw it as a last resort.

Steve went to counseling on his own and began taking steps to show Kim how much he truly cared. One of the first things he did was write his wife a long, heartfelt love letter.

Kim shared the letter with some of her friends who remarked at how beautiful it was. But Steve's words of love and devotion had no effect on Kim.

"Can you believe this shit?" Kim mocked as she read some passages aloud. "I am willing to do whatever it takes to save our marriage. It takes two of us. But I know we can do it. Together."

"I think that's sweet," her friend remarked.

"Gag me," Kim rolled her eyes. "Trust me, when you've been married as long as I have this kind of syrupy shit only makes you sick."

"I wish my husband would write me love letters."

"No," Kim said. "You don't. They keep coming and they don't stop. He's smothering me and following me around the house like a puppy dog."

Steve's renewed efforts to rekindle a long dead marriage were now being met with resentment. He was earnest in displaying his affection and becoming more communicative with Kim.

"Let's talk about our feelings," he said to his wife who stiffened with his every touch.

Kim would go to work eager to vent. She would open up about her marital difficulties to anyone who was willing to listen. She found a confidante in Jennifer Gowen.

"He is suffocating me," Kim told Gowen. "Stifling me. Following me around the damn house the whole time and cuddling with me at night. I can't even breathe. He's always asking me where I'm going or what I'm doing. Now he's calling me on my cell just to say 'Hi'. He never used to do that. It is annoying as shit."

But Steve was merely following the advise of his counsel. He had not dated much before Kim and she was his first serious relationship. He had no idea what to do when the relationship turned sour.

"It has to be said that Steve was on the receiving end of some very bad counseling advice," Orange said. "Appeasement never works and that is something that any decent psychiatrist or counselor should know. He kept turning the other cheek with Kim and that just fueled her resentment of him even more. This isn't to justify his murder, of course."

With his counseling session inspired efforts not yielding any results, Steve became distraught. He had done everything by the book but it wasn't working. He called his close friend Mike and opened up about his marriage and job difficulties.

"I don't know what to do, man," Steve said, his voice quaking with emotion. "I don't want to lose her. She's my life. My family is my everything. I feel like I've already lost her."

"Take it easy," Mike said. "We'll figure something out."

"What do you think I should do?" Steve asked.

"You need to take her out," Mike said "Someplace special. You know. Make a memory."

"Yeah," Steve said. "I know that. But I'm at a loss at how to go about it. I've tried everything."

"Tell you what," Mike said. "You come over to the Golf Resort."

"Harbourtowne?"

"I'll make sure you get the honeymoon cottage we have here. The very best one."

"You're too cool, Mike."

"Anytime, brother."

Mike worked at the Harbourtowne Golf Resort and set up the accommodations for his good friend and his wife. The place was hosting a Valentine's Day Murder Mystery play. Mike knew that the place worked wonders for romance. If there was anyplace that could rekindle the spark in a relationship, the resort would be it.

But Steve didn't know that Kim already had a romance of her own.

His name was Brad Winkler.

CHAPTER THREE

Kim had met Brad Winkler when she was planning out the bachelorette party for her co-worker, Jennifer Gowen. Jennifer had brought Brad to the wedding shower ahead of time and the United States Marine was the only man at the party aside from Steve.

Kim and the young man hit it off immediately. She gave him a ride home along with Norma Walz after the party was over. They dropped off Brad at his aunt's house and Kim watched from the car as the young man made his way inside.

"He was in a bad marriage," Kim said to Norma. "Pretty sad. He's a nice guy. Jesus. The girl who catches him is going to be a lucky one. He's really sweet."

Kim returned home and was chastised by Steve for spending so much time with Brad. He had no idea of the affair to come.

Jennifer Gowen would get married and enlist the aid of Brad to help around the house while she was away on her honeymoon. Jennifer had a one-year-old daughter and Brad would babysit the girl and do some chores around the place.

Kim would come over and help out with the baby on the day Gowen left.

The affair with Brad would begin that night. They would have their trysts at Jen's townhouse while his cousin was still on her honeymoon. When Jennifer returned, the couple would continue their affair at the home of Brad's aunt.

Kim was equally open about her affair with Brad Winkler among friends as she was about her dissatisfaction with her marriage.

"I'm seeing someone," Kim said to Rachel, her college friend.

"You're having an affair?"

"Its just sex," Kim said, shrugging her shoulder. "I'm not going to marry this guy."

Kim kept up the charade on the home front as she plotted her next move. The change in her behavior made Steve believe that his efforts were working as he chronicled in his journal.

"Life at home is improving," Steve wrote. "I am looking forward to Valentine's weekend at Harbourtowne with Kim. She called twice today and said 'I love you' without me saying it first. I was very happy. Kim and I have not made love yet and I want to but I will wait as long as it takes. I love her...I believe I know what being in love really is. We have been married nine years but I feel like we just started dating."

Sadly, four days after Steve wrote those words in his journal Kim was off buying Brad Winkler a Valentine's Day gift.

"Brad, I really want to give you all these gifts in person but I guess the Pentagon had a different idea," Kim wrote. "I am so proud of what you do so I'll just go on missing you. Have a nice weekend at home, baby. I look forward to seeing you soon. Happy Valentine's Day, sir. I love you so very much. Hugs and Kisses, Kim."

While Steve had an optimistic view of their future life together, Kim continued to tell anyone with a listening ear about her dissatisfaction.

"There is a lot of verbal abuse," Kim said to Theresa Armstrong, one of her neighbors. "From both of us. He doesn't do anything. I do everything. I am unhappy and don't want to be married to him anymore."

She then went to her job at Holy Cross Hospital and told her co-worker Norma Walz about her problems.

"I've been in a bad marriage for a long time," Kim said. "Me and Steve have been having problems for a long time. A very long time."

"I always suspected that something wasn't right," Norma said.

"I've been living a lie," Kim nodded. I wanted him to go to counseling two years ago. Now he's going. And he's driving me crazy."

Steve's constant fawning and pandering annoyed Kim so much that she began thinking about what life would be like without him.

"You know if my husband dies we'd be better off than if we got a divorce," Kim told one of her neighbors. "Steve doesn't make that much money. He's a groundskeeper. We get a divorce and I'm paying him alimony. But if he died, well, if he died we would inherit $450,000 from his life insurance."

"That's a morbid thing to think about," the neighbor said, trying to laugh it off.

"You read about these stories all the time. The husband killing off the wife and vice-versa. I always wondered why they did it instead of just getting a divorce. It's the life insurance. Just like in the movies."

"What was lost in Kim's rationalizing was the fact that the killers most always get caught," Orange said. "But in her mind, she was the special one. Narcissists always think like that. Like they are the special one that won't get caught. Still, Kim needed that reassurance from her peers that she was doing the right thing as crazy as it sounds."

After not getting a receptive response from her neighbor, Kim once again turned to Jennifer Gowen.

"Steve would be better off dead," Kim said, using the same line on Jennifer. "We talked about getting a divorce but Steve doesn't want that. Even if he did he is going to try and turn Anna against me or try to keep her. He doesn't have a life outside our marriage so he is better off dead anyway."

"You really shouldn't talk like that. Let alone think like that."

"Why not? I thought about telling him about Brad but I think he would just get depressed or suicidal. Then I would not be able to collect the insurance if he killed himself."

"You think he'd kill himself?"

"Probably," Kim said. "So I have to figure something else out. You know there was this serial killer. I forgot her name. But she would go around in the children's ward and shoot the kids up with Succinylcholine. It is a muscle paralyzer. No way to trace it."

Kim would later inform Gowen that if she could kill Steve and get away with it that she "would do it tomorrow."

Seeking other alternatives aside from poisoning, Kim approached fellow surgical tech Ken Burges in the locker room of the hospital.

"Hi, Ken."

"Hey there," Ken said.

"Do you know of anyone that could kill my husband?"

"What?" Ken asked. He thought Kim was playing a joke.

"Do you know anyone that can, you know, kill someone? For a price."

"I'm insulted that you would ask me that. Do I look that sketchy to you?"

Burges had been convicted of welfare fraud in Virginia a couple of years before obtaining his job at the hospital. Because of this, Kim may have presumed that he would be the type of person who would know people capable of such an act.

"I got $50,000 for anyone who could do something like that."

"You got the wrong dude," Ken said. "The wrong guy."

"Forget I even asked," Kim said.

"You work in the operating room," Ken advised. "You could just put him to sleep."

Ken didn't know that Kim already had that idea in mind.

Kim began to plot out details of the murder. She needed to do something that was untraceable. This called for poison. She had to burn away any evidence so her attack had to take place away from home.

She ran her plan by a college friend of hers, Rachel McCoy. Kim justified her actions by demonizing her husband. She talked about his unwillingness to do stuff with her as he was a homebody and kept a messy home. Their personalities were too different.

Then without warning, she began articulating her plan to kill Steve with the poison and then setting the place on fire.

It was almost as if she wanted Rachel to poke any holes in her plan should she miss anything.

Rachel tried to talk Kim out of the hare-brained idea to no avail. She suggested simply getting a divorce but Kim was convinced that killing Steve was "easier." Rachel also brought up the fact that she was robbing their daughter, Anna, of a father.

"She would be better off without him," Kim said.

Whatever Rachel suggested, Kim had an answer for.

Her mind was made up.

Steve had to go.

CHAPTER FOUR

Kim knew that the drug she had to obtain was Succinylcholine. It would be readily available to her as she did her rounds through the hospital. Just walk by a tray of meds in the surgery unit and lift one of the vials. Easy peasy.

"I'm going to get this drug," Kim told her friend Rachel. "It will paralyze Steve. Stop his breathing and then I'll set the curtains on fire with a candle or a cigar. He won't be able to move and then he'll die of smoke inhalation. Nobody will know shit."

Kim would not take into account the fact that her husband was a healthy and robust man with no medical history. That would certainly draw suspicion.

"This would be the only logical explanation for what brought about Steven Hricko's death," prosecuting attorney Robert Dean said. "Because there was nothing else wrong with him. His body organs were in fine shape, there was no trauma. It had to have been this. She had to have carried through her plan."

"Kim was determined," Orange said. "She wanted her cake and eat it too. It is a head scratcher as to why she didn't pursue a divorce but the mind of a sociopath works differently. She wanted a clean break. If she had gotten a divorce, then Steve would have remained in her life forever the next ten years because of their daughter. She wanted to erase him from the picture and nothing and nobody was going to talk her out of it."

The planned romantic getaway loomed on the horizon for Valentine's Day weekend. Steve looked forward to their alone time together with giddy excitement. He told his counselor that this would be the turning point where the sparks of romance would once again be rekindled.

But Kim looked toward the weekend with dread. She had told Jennifer Gowen that she had only had sex with Steve once in the past six months and the experience left her feeling repulsed.

"I'm not looking forward to the trip," Kim said in her own counseling session.

"Why?" her counselor asked. "It may be an opportunity to rekindle some passion."

"I'm tired and really don't feel up to the trip. It's a long drive. It is going to be miserable."

Then a light bulb flashed in Kim's mind. The resort would be the perfect place.

The perfect place to put her plans into effect.

CHAPTER SIX

Valentine's Day weekend arrived.

Steve had romance on his mind. His forehead perspired as he felt the anxiety of trying to save his marriage.

Kim had Brad Winkler on her mind as she looked out the car window.

Then her mind drifted to murder.

She had to set everything up just right. Inject Steve. Burn the cottage room. Then tell the police her story and stick with it no matter what.

Kim and Steve drove from their home in Laurel, Maryland to St Michaels. It would be a 75-mile to a romantic getaway that many had christened as the "Heart & Soul of Chesapeake Bay."

But the couple arrived at their cottage and found the place to be freezing. Kim started a fire in the wood stove then made some coffee.

The conversation was muted and awkward. They decided to watch some TV before looking out the window and taking in the view of the bay. It was windy and the the cold, damp weather chased them back inside

Preparing for the dinner, Steve popped a few Effexor tablets for his depression which had gotten worse in recent weeks. He also took an anti-anxiety medication called Xanax and a muscle relaxant called Flexeril.

Getting dressed, they attended the interactive murder mystery dinner called THE BRIDE WHO CRIED. The actors staged a re-enactment of a woman killing her soon to be husband. The actors encouraged audience members to ask the actors questions in an attempt to find out who the murderer was.

Kim enjoyed the play immensely. When the actors called for audience participation, she was one of two women who went out onto the stage and began asking questions like a detective.

The play now over, Kim and Steve returned to their cottage. Not yet having their fill of entertainment, the couple would watch the comedy film "Tommy Boy". They got a good laugh out of it but according to Kim they "still did not talk about our problems."

Steve then fell asleep.

Kim stood over him like a predator then went to the bathroom to prepare her lethal cocktail of succinylcholine. Building up her nerve, she finally did the move that she had been practicing in her head for two years.

Kim pulled aside the bed sheet and injected the syringe into his neck.

I'll burn the body. That will get rid of the puncture wound.

Kim also knew that the drug she administered only caused paralysis. It didn't affect a patient's level of consciousness.

So when Kim set the room on fire, Steve would know that he was being burned to death.

And he wouldn't be able to do anything about it.

The thought made Kim smile. She didn't want to just kill him. She wanted to make him suffer. To humiliate him.

Kim pulled the now paralyzed but awake Steve off the bed and dropped him to the floor. She doused his body with lighter fluid.

Kim, what are you doing? Steve looked up at his wife, unable to move or speak.

"Call it the perfect crime," she whispered in his ear as if reading his thoughts.

He stared straight up at the ceiling, catching Kim's movements in the corner of his eye.

He heard a matchstick strike against a box.

Then he felt a sharp pain race up his body as she set him ablaze.

I can't move, Steven thought as terror and pain engulfed him.

I can't breathe.

I can't breathe.

Kim, what are you doing?

I brought you here to save our marriage. I have done what I could do making this better.

I love you. Please don't do this!

Kim poured more of the lighter fluid onto Steve's body. She lit another match and threw it on him.

"She injected him with succinylcholine and watched him suffocate," Maureen said. "And lit him on fire. How much colder could it get."

CHAPTER FIVE

Kim Hricko walked into the resort reception area with a calm demeanor. She had her ear to her cell phone which was turned upside down.

"I need to talk to someone who works here," she informed desk clerk Elaine Phillips.

"I work here," Elaine said, expecting Kim's response being anything from wanting more towels to complaining about faulty air conditioning.

"My room is on fire."

"Is there anyone else in the room?" Phillips asked.

"Yeah," she said without emotion. "My husband."

"What room are you in?" Elaine asked, making her way around the corner of the desk.

Elaine and another hotel employee hurried into the courtyard of the resort.

"You smell that?" Elaine asked. "Something is definitely burning."

The two sprinted to cottage number 506 at the end of the resort. The door was shut but there was a tiny opening in the sliding door in the rear.

Smoke filled the room. They could barely see one foot in front of them. Kneeling down, one of the employees saw the

the prone figure of a man inside. He crawled in, braving the smoke and pulled the body to safety on the back porch.

It was too late.

Steve Hricko, burned to a crisp.

The man had died with a Playboy magazine at his side with his pajama pants down at his knees as if he collapsed while masturbating.

"I want to see his dead body," Kim said as she milled around with the hotel guests watching the scene.

"I thought it was odd," one of the guests said. "Because no one had pronounced anyone to be dead yet."

Kim gave her statement to the Sheriff then called their best friends, Mike and Maureen Miller.

"It's the last thing you expect when you receive a phone call at night," Maureen said. "When the phone rings at night you know that it's not anything good."

"My wife answered the phone," Mike Miller said. "And sort of roused me a little bit and said that there's was an incident in Steve and Kim's room. Kim's requesting that you come down there as soon as possible.

The Millers were shocked at the sudden death of Steve. They were even more shocked at the demeanor of Kim when they went to console her.

"I didn't expect her to be anything less than a hysterical woman whose husband passed away," Maureen said. "She was the exact opposite. Just exact opposite."

Kim told everyone that Steve was drunk and made advances toward her. He groped and fondled her but she didn't want to have sex. They argued and she left the cottage.

Mike knew that something was fishy. His friend Steve was not a drinker.

Did Kim plan this out?

"They said the fire started because of him carelessly smoking," Mike said. "Steve doesn't smoke. All the years I've known Steve, I've never seen him smoke a cigarette, a cigar. He despised being around people that smoked."

An autopsy was performed and forensic pathologist Janis Amatuzio, like Mike Miller, quickly realized that something was amiss.

"Steven's body was found in a fire," Amatuzio said. "The major question for the forensic pathologist is that did he die of the fire or not. When there was no soot in the airways, when there was no damage to the lungs. It suggested that Steven was dead before the fire started."

"Steven was not drunk that night," prosecuting attorney Robert Dean said. "The drug tests and the autopsy shows that. Steve was not drunk."

The picture didn't fit. Steve was not a drinker nor was he a smoker. But friends and family could not believe the worst about Kim Hricko. The fun and outgoing mother could not have killed her own husband, the man who adored her for the past nine years.

Could she?

"Was she really capable of doing this?" Maureen asked. "Everybody was saying it but again, I ignored it and just pushed it back and said that she wasn't capable of doing it. Man, was I wrong."

CHAPTER SIX

Police began their investigation and discovered that Kim left a trail of incriminating conversations as well as evidence.

"Kim was too smart for her own good," Orange said. "She did her research on succinylcholine, did her research on the how quickly a body burns. But she did not know how to stage a killing."

Kim had left empty beer bottles in the room and a pack of cigars. The cigars would be the clue that blew Kim's story up in smoke.

Steve was not a smoker and the cigars she had left behind as evidence were not the kind to start a fire.

"There was an investigation as to how a fire like this could have started," prosecuting attorney Robert Dean said. "That fire could not have started by the ashes of a cigar."

Kim would state that after she and Steve had gotten into a fight she went for a drive. She wanted to visit Mike and Maureen Miller who only lived minutes away. She stated she had become lost. The prosecution thought that her excuse seemed odd as she had visited the Millers on numerous occasions. She also had a brother who lived only a few blocks away from the Miller home. And why had she not simply called them on her cell phone?

"I didn't want to wake anyone," Kim said when asked why she didn't call.

Her answer was incongruent as why would she worry about waking someone up with a cell phone call when she didn't have a problem arriving on their doorstep in the middle of the night?

Nine days after the murder, police would arrive at the home of a Hricko friend where Kim had been staying. They had a search warrant for her car but Kim felt the noose tightening around her neck. She ran to the bathroom room and locked it behind herself as the police entered the home.

Kim then swallowed a whole bottle of Xanax.

"Come out of there, Kim," the police yelled.

They busted the door down and saw Kim there in the bathtub, holding a razor blade over her wrist.

"I'll kill myself!" she screamed. "I'll fucking do it!"

The officers quickly subdued Kim without further incident. They then transported her to a psychiatric facility where she was put on suicide watch.

The trial would only last six days as the prosecuting attorney detailed how Kim staged the murder.

"She stated that he was sloppy drunk," prosecuting attorney Robert Dean said. "And that he wanted to have sex. She said they got into an argument and that she left for a few hours. She said she drove around and got lost. And then she returned to the cottage and saw that it was full of smoke and then she reported that the room was on fire."

The case against Kim was made by several friends, co-workers, and neighbors. They all testified about the affair, the plot to kill Steve and her desire to acquire the drug succinylcholine.

Kim Hricko would be found guilty of murder and arson. She would be sentenced to life in prison.

"It's sad that he (Steve) is not the one in the world anymore and she is," Maureen said.

"He was my best friend," Mike said. "And the fact that he isn't here anymore is pretty hard for me to take."

The other victim aside from Steve was their nine-year-old daughter. She lost both her father and her mother.

"Her child is the victim," Maureen said. "And is forever going to wonder which side of the family is telling the truth. Is it true that her mother was unjustly accused or is it true that she's a cold, manipulating, calculating murderer."

END

DANA SUE GRAY

84

KAREN COLLIER

Dana Sue Gray was born on December 6th, 1957 in Pasadena, California. Her mother, Beverly Arnett, was a former beauty queen who worked as a professional model. Her father, Russell Armbrust, worked as a hairdresser and was married three times prior to marrying Beverly. The couple had several miscarriages before Dana was born.

Her mother was born for the camera and loved attention. She liked being pampered, getting her make-up done and wearing flashy outfits. Beverly modeled for Bullock's, did print ads for Hamilton watches and was once a Rose Princess at the Tournament of Roses Parade.

LIKE MOTHER LIKE DAUGHTER

Russell divorced Beverly, however, when he witnessed his wife attack an older woman that had angered her. Beverly had also maxed out his credit cards, putting him financial peril. Dana was only two years old at the time of the divorce and rarely saw her father.

"Some kind of estrangement had taken place," forensic psychologist Lora Dixon said. "After her parents divorced she had turned down invitations in her teen years to visit her father on all of the holidays and birthday get-togethers."

"There is also something to think about here in terms of Beverly's own temper. Dana clearly witnessed violence and bullying from her mother at an early age. She inherited those characteristics from her mother with tragic results."

Dana had discipline problems early on as she sought attention from her narcissistic mother. Her mother would discipline her but Dana would retaliate by stealing money to buy candy. Her mother had two other children from a previous marriage. Dana would go into the rooms of her step brothers and urinate in their beds.

Her mother would continue to try and discipline her to no avail as Dana would lash back with violence. This facet of her personality was never placed under her control.

"Mommy and daughter didn't get along," Dixon said. "But obviously that isn't unusual nor does mean she was destined to become a serial killer. There was some deep seated issues festering here though. This is evident when Dana gave her mother a snake for Christmas. 'A snake for a snake' the card must have read."

Nonetheless, it did not appear on the surface that Dana had to endure the brutal childhood that gave birth to so many other serial killers. Cedric Ward, one of her step brothers, did admit that Dana did not have the best of childhoods. "It was not happy growing up," he recalled.

SCHOOL AND SEX

Dana did not get along with other students and achieved low grades in all of her classes. She was a chronic truancy case and often forged notes to get out of class. Dara was sexually active at a very early age as she would lose her virginity at the age of twelve. She would ultimately go from one relationship to the next, using sex to lure men into her web of narcissism.

"Dana has a problem," said Richard Singer, a boyfriend of her mother. "She does not want to be told no. She has her own thing, and nobody could tell her any different. You could not tell Dana what to do."

"Her mother would pretty much try to control her, but Dana would go off on you. You could not tell her what to do. Dana is very hyperactive and opinionated."

During her adolescent years, she loved horror movies and read Grimm's Fairy Tales numerous times. As a teenager, she and a neighbor built a catapult. They would tie tiny parachutes on the cat's backs and then hurl them into the air, with the parachute carrying them down into neighborhood swimming pools.

A MOTHER'S DEATH

Beverly contracted breast cancer when Dana was fourteen. Dana decided to become a nurse after witnessing the way the nurses at the hospital treated her mother. Her mother died and Dana was forced back to live with her father.

"The temptation here is to say that Dana was inspired to become a nurse by witnessing the compassion the nurses shown her mother during her illness," Dixon said. "But I would posit a different psychological scenario. Dana saw that the nurses had power over her mother. That for once, her mother was weak and had to defer to other people for the first time in her life. Dana wanted power. Control. What better way to get that then to become a nurse?"

Dana went into a depression after her mother died and would reveal her sentimentality in letters she would write to her then boyfriend, Don Lane, in jail.

"Tomorrow, Good Friday, 4-1-94, is also April Fool's and also my real mom's 76th B-day. It's been 22 years since her death, and I still celebrate her B-day for her. I celebrate it for her 'cause she died when I was 14 and we never got to get past the 'grow years' to become friends like my dad and I are. She was wild-but made my younger years a total adventure: camping, clamming @ Pismo, best Halloween parties and the best Xmases a poor family could have. She could make a fun time out of just anything."

"Again, you see in her letters a sense of victimhood," Dixon said. "She makes no mention of her mother ignoring her birthdays. And she describes her family as 'poor.' They lived in relatively affluent area, becoming strapped for cash primarily because of Beverly's spending."

GROWING UP

Dana's father Russell had remarried, living with his new wife Yvonne who had a daughter named Cathy. Dana would move in with the couple, sharing a room with Cathy. The reunion between her and her father would be a short-lived one, however, as Yvonne would find marijuana in Dana's room.

Russell's wife then kicked Dana out of the home.

On her own at the age of fifteen, Dana would move-in with her sky-diving instructor, Rob Beaudry. The union would produce two pregnancies but Rob talked Dana in to getting abortions both times. These were decisions that she would later come to resent.

At five-foot-two and weighing a stocky 135 lbs, Dana would nonetheless inherit her mother's penchant for fancy clothes and desire to be pampered with manicures and pedicures. Despite her taste in high-end living, associates would describe her appearance and demeanor as "hard."

She would graduate from Newport High School in 1976 and enter nursing school at Saddleback College in Mission Viejo, California. Dana paid her way through nursing school while working as waitress. She also taught herself screen printing techniques and sold screen printed items for extra cash.

"Dana inherited her mother's psychology when it came to money and relationships," Dixon said. "She operated from a 'lack mindset', in that she always saw herself as poor. She was industrious but felt sorry for herself that she had to work so hard, paying her way through school and working for a living. The shopping sprees were a relief to her perceived burden."

ESTRANGED FROM FAMILY

Dana became estranged from her half-brothers, her older siblings from Beverly's previous marriage. The reasons were always financial as she become embroiled in a dispute over the proceedings from their aunt's estate.

She had run-ins with her half-brother Rick in particular.

Dana reacted with anger after he told her to sell belongings to pay her mounting bills. Rick wrote back telling her that she had no consideration for others.

"Nuts," is how her sister-in-law described her. "Not even normally greedy. Crazy. Gray is missing a conscience. I do not think it is there. When you talk to her, she has no concept of other human beings."

"The half-brothers clearly knew she was trouble," Dixon said. "They did the right thing in distancing themselves.

NURSING CAREER.

Immediately upon graduating from Saddleback, Dana landed a nursing job at Corona Community Hospital. She used that as a springboard to a high paying position as an operating room nurse at Inland Valley Regional Medical Center (some reports have her identified as a labor and delivery nurse). She was described by one nursing supervisor as "very caring."

During this time, she had found another boyfriend, a windsurfer whom she would accompany on trips to Hawaii where they would pursue various outdoor activities. This relationship would be an on-again, off-again type deal until Dana would marry Tom Gray. The couple would tie the knot at a winery in the affluent Temecula area.

Tom was an active sportsman and had a crush on Dana since high school.

"She was a hard core athlete," Tom recalled. "A sky diver, wind surfer, mountain bike enthusiast and snorkeler, and she was skilled in each sport."

Dana took pride in her physical strength and would often roll up her sleeve to reveal her bicep muscle. 'She how strong I am?' she would ask.

Living in the gated community of the affluent Canyon Lake suited Dana as it would have been something that would have pleased her mother. Her and Tom started numerous businesses where they used the name "Graymatter."

Tom could not stop Dana's spending habits, however. The couple took out a loan for $47,000 and another for $20,000 within the first nine months of their marriage.

"She was replicating the marriage of her mother and father," Dixon said. "She liked the empowerment that came from having a lot of money. Having money, or rather the act of spending money is what fed her ego. Only in Dana's case she took it way beyond her mother. She was willing to kill for that feeling."

The marriage quickly soured when Dana's spending habits sent the couple into overwhelming consumer debt. Her alcoholism also worsened, particularly after she suffered a miscarriage. Dana indulged in three or four glasses of wine while cooking dinner and then having more with the dinner itself. Her days off from the hospital were adventures in bourbon whiskey, 7-Up and Tequila shooters. Later, she would admit to using marijuana and cocaine.

When Gray unexpectedly received a $7500 inheritance, Dana took the money and blew it on a trip to Europe, leaving her husband behind at home. When she returned , she began an affair with Don Lane, a musician in her husband's band. When Lane agreed to support her, she moved out of the Canyon Lake house and spent $11,000 in five months.

In March of 1992, however, Dana began seeing a psychiatrist. He prescribed Paxil for her, probably to stave off depression among other things.

Lane had a five year old son at the time and would later tell authorities of Dana's "mood changes" and her propensity to break out into "hysterical tears" with little provocation.

She filed for divorce from Tom but this would not be finalized until much later. In September of 1993, Tom and Dana were forced to file for bankruptcy to prevent foreclosure on their Canyon Lake residence.

Despite the value of the home increasing, the amount they owed on the house was more than its worth. They owed $177,500 on a house valued at $125,000 because of double mortgages.

She suffered a miscarriage, exacerbating more depression as well as alcohol and drug abuse.

FIRED FROM THE HOSPITAL

The trouble continued for Dana as two months later she would be fired from the hospital for stealing Demerol and other opiate pain killers.

"What Dana was trying to do was medicate herself," Dixon said. "The new marriage, the exotic vacations, the fancy house and cars. It was never enough to quell the demons that spoke in her head. A control freak out of control. So she struggled to constantly fill the void with booze and drugs. Then this spirals into an affair with a friend of her husband. Again, this life trajectory happens to a lot of people. In Dana's case, however, she needed that extra thrill. Something more than the rush of sky-diving, cheating on her husband, and getting high. She needed the ultimate adrenaline rush. The power to take someone's life."

TIME TO KILL

In later reports, hospital authorities would reveal their own problems with Gray.

"She is sarcastic," Darlena Addison, the former nursing supervisor who fired Gray for stealing drugs. "She does get her point across if she's crossed or doesn't get her way."

"The problem was a condescending attitude, as Dana believed that she was smarter than everyone and had a need to dominate."

The hospital would later report that they did not have any "unusual" deaths during Gray's tenure.

"Of course that is what you would expect them to say," Dixon said. "If they admit to any 'unusual' deaths then it certainly opens them up to a lawsuit. The opportunity would certainly be there for Dana to steal credit cards from elderly patients and rack up bills. It appears, however, that she did not put her murderous impulses into action until after her dismissal. Dana fell in love with the struggle. The fight of her victim as long as she would emerge on he winning end. Poisoning her victims to death in the way it would have been possible for her as a nurse would not have given her that adrenaline rush."

After the loss of her job, Dana would amp up her indulgences in alcohol, drinking straight Vodka, loving the Smirnoff brand in particular.

On Valentine's Day in 1994, Dana contacted Tom's parents (after their separation he had kept his phone number and address a secret). She informed Tom's parents that she wanted to meet with him.

Tom agreed at first but later did not show up.

Tom would find out that Dana had taken out an insurance policy on him without his knowledge. The policy payout would have been enough to pay down the Canyon Lake home the couple used to share.

Later that day, Dana murdered Norma Davis.

THE FIRST VICTIM

Norma Davis was 86 years old at the time. She was the mother-in-law of the woman (Jeri Davis Armbrust) who married Dana's father in 1988. Jeri's first husband, Bill Davis, was Norma's son. Bill died in the early 1980s, and his widow married a newly divorced Russell.

But Jeri continued to care for her elderly mother-in-law, even after she remarried. Dana would also come to know Norma very well.

On February 16th, 1994, however, the body of Norma Davis would be found by a neighbor named Alice Williams. She had been dead for two days as someone had stabbed her in the neck with a wood-handled utility knife. The blade had been inserted so deep that it nearly severed Norma's head.

She also had a filet knife sticking out of her chest.

Police would discover no forced entry into the home. Norma always kept the doors locked unless she was expecting a visitor. Her neighbor, Alice, stated that she could not remember if Norma had mentioned she was expecting company.

"We didn't have a lot of information," Detective Joe Greco said. "The only piece of evidence that we had was the entry way of the condominium. There was a faint shoe print on the condominium and it was a 6 ½ size shoe."

Detectives would find the Nike shoe print and Davis' Social Security check in plain view. Additionally, on the first floor of the condo, they found a smear of blood on an armchair and a torn phone cord.

A modus operandi had been established. Dana would manually strangle her victims with a phone cord, then use an object to smash or stab.

The coroner concluded that Norma Davis was strangled first then stabbed. She was stabbed eleven times with Dana leaving the knives stuck in her body.

Police described the scene as one of the most brutal they had ever encountered.

"It was a shock because it was only my second homicide case as a detective," Greco said. "It was overwhelming. It crossed my mind that I had a serial killer on my hands."

SHE DEVIL ON A RAMPAGE

"The community was very affluent," Greco said. "They don't have a lot of homicides."

On February 28th, 1994, 66-year old June Roberts was found murdered. She had lived in the gated community of Canyon Lake along with Dana.

Dana had known Roberts and visited her that day saying that she wanted to borrow a book about either overcoming alcohol addiction or vitamins, the reports vary. Dana had her boyfriend's five year old son waiting out in front in her Cadillac.

Ignorant of Dana's true motives, Roberts allowed Dana into her home. She went to retrieve the book Dana inquired about while her would-be killer ripped out the cords to June's phone

Dana would later describe their interaction taking a turn when she became "really annoyed" that June came back with the wrong book. She also told a psychologist that she became infuriated that June allegedly said that she "didn't do enough" to save her marriage with Tom.

When asked what made Dana believe that Roberts and her other victims were looking down on her, Dana responded that she did not like their body language.

"The arching of the eyebrow," Dana said. "That is what happened. All three."

Dana then used the phone cord to strangle Roberts to death.

"I was right behind her," Dana recalled. "I choked her with the phone cord. She was holding on, trying to get the cord off. I pulled her down. She was on her back. I hit her in the head with a bottle. I lost it. I was so consumed. I don't know the time span in there-must have been very quick. She must have stopped moving, and I left. As I walked out, she had a little wallet thing. I grabbed it."

"We went out and proceeded to shop up a storm. "

In talking to psychologists,.Dana appeared unaware of the concept of remorse.

"It was very brutal," Greco said. "The victim had been strangled with her own telephone cord and actually tied to a chair. And she was struck so hard (by the wine bottle) she fractured her skull."

Her autopsy noted a "moderately deep ligature furrow" and a "6 x 3 purple contusion." The cranium contusion was caused by a heavy glass wine bottle striking her with tremendous force. The volume of blood in and near the bathroom door, the walls and pooling under the body made it impossible to gauge the age of the victim.

"This is when the profile of Dana Sue becomes highly unusual," Dixon said. "With female serial killers, you usually see poison or the use of a gun as the weapon of choice. Dana Sue, however, approached her victims with a high level of physical violence that rivaled a male serial killer. There was nothing lady-like about her approach. She was a cold blooded, hands on killer."

TIME TO SHOP

Dana did not hesitate after murdering Roberts, she had to get her shopping fix met.

She would go to Bally's Wine Country Cafe in Temecula, eat crab cake and scampi while charging the meal to Robert's credit card. She could not finish the entire meal, however, and had the waitress pack the rest.

She then got an eyebrow wax and a perm then treated her boyfriend's son to a stylish haircut.

"The fact that she had the little boy accompany her on both the murders and the shopping trips deserves mention," Dixon said. "Dana remained childless throughout life. She was regretted getting two abortions and suffered a miscarriage during her marriage with Tom. Going out and about with her boyfriend's son made her feel like a Mommy. She could be the Mommy that she never had, treating the young child to things she always wanted."

Dana signed "June Roberts" on the $164.76 charge at the salon. She then went to the mall and spent $511 on a black suede jacket, several pairs of cowboy boots, and then $161 on a pair of diamond earrings all charged to Roberts. Her addiction still not satiated, she went to a drug store, picking up dog treats, two bottles of Smirnoff and a toy police helicopter for the boy.

The day after, Dana loaded up on suntan lotion, got a massage at Murrieta Hot Springs resort and then went on another power shopping spree.

"She had absolutely no remorse," Dixon said. "There was no hiding out and laying low like some other wimpy male serial killer. Dana Sue was different. She killed and then she had to do the one thing that gratified her. She had to get to the mall. She had to get the high from buying stuff. She had to enjoy the power while it still lasted."

Ironically, none of her victims had anything stolen aside from their credit cards.

"Dana didn't take any rings from her victims," Greco said. "Or some valuables from the home that were obvious. So I don't think any of the crimes were motivated by money."

Ten days after the Roberts' murder, Dana would enter an antique store, the Main Street Trading Post in Lake Elsinore. Dana stated to the cashier, Dorinda Hawkins, that she wanted to buy a picture frame for a photo of her deceased mother.

"Dana came in asking about picture frames," Greco said. "During their interaction, Dana felt that Dorinda was being condescending to her.

"I felt sick to my stomach," Dana said. "I wanted to vomit. I wanted her to die."

Dana asked if Hawkins was working alone and then she attacked her, strangling her with the store's telephone cord.

"Dorinda is begging for her life when Dana is strangling her," Greco said. "And Dorinda told her 'you can have anything you want. Take the cash, I have eight kids, just let me live.' And Dana told her 'I'm not doing this for the money.' She said that twice. And that really gives you an insight on what Dana is thinking while she's committing these crimes."

Dorinda, however, continued to fight, resisting Dana all the way.

"Relax," Dana said, trying to coax Hawkins into dying. "Just relax."

Hawkins grabbed a broom and poked Dana with it to no avail.

Dana then shoved Hawkins to the ground and stepped on her head as a brace to better choke her.

"Her eyes were flat," Hawkins recalled. "I could tell she had killed before."

Believing her victim dead, Dana stole five dollars from Hawkins' purse and twenty dollars from the cash register.

An hour later, she began another shopping spree, still using Roberts' credit cards.

Hawkins, however, would survive the attack and provide the police the required description of Dana.

THE ATTACKS CONTINUE

Nearly a month after her first killing, on March 16th, 1994, Dana would kill the 87-year old Dora Beebe.

Moments after Beebe arrived home from a doctor's appointment, Dana pulled up in front of her house. She knocked on the door and asked Beebe for directions.

"Here we see Dana getting bolder," Dixon said. "With Norma Davis and June Roberts, she knew the victims beforehand. And the attempted murder in the antique store seemed to be a spur of the moment thing. But the Beebe murder is the first occasion where Dana has picked out a stranger. Elderly women were her preferred target, specifically those who were alone, and tragically Beebe emerged in her cross-hairs."

Living in the same neighborhood for several years, it was improbable for Dana to become lost. But she used that as an excuse when she came knocking on Beebe's door asking for directions.

Dana became angry when Beebe said "I don't have time for this." She was able to hide her anger as Beebe capitulated and allowed Dana insider her home to look at a map. Once inside the home, however, Dana assaulted the elderly woman.

'She turned her back on me," Dana said. "I choked her with the phone cord. I hit her in the head with an iron. As I remember it, it wasn't much of a fight."

Using a stainless steel Black and Decker iron that Dana found in the home, Dana bashed Beebe in the head so hard that it dented the appliance.

Less then an hour later, Dana would be at the mall with Beebe's credit cards in hand.

"She enjoyed doing things that were risky," Greco said. "She was a thrill seeker. I think that she really enjoyed what she was doing. She got a thrill out of it."

PANIC IN THE STREETS

The residents in the gated community of Canyon Lake went into panic mode. Some of the elderly citizens moved in with family until the killer was caught. A group of elderly widows organized themselves to sleep together at designated houses, not wanting to be alone.

There were some who thought the killings where the product of a cult engaging in the ritual sacrifice of the elderly.

"Rumors circulated around the entire community," Dixon said. "A terrifying time for everyone, the elderly in particular. This was a relatively well-to-do neighborhood. People were unused to killings, let alone a serial killer. Numerous people bought guns and kept it by their bedside while others banded together in the belief that there were safety in numbers."

FALSE SUSPECT

Police detectives were at a loss early on in finding a suspect. Prospects were so bleak that a supervisor in charge had seriously thought about using a psychic. Dana was not anywhere near the police's list of possible killers. Instead, the police initially suspected that her mother-in-law, Jeri Armbrust, might be the killer.

The police determined that Armbrust used to be married to Davis' son and continued to care for her former mother-in-law.

Detectives grew suspicious because it was unusual that Jeri would continue to take care of someone who was not a blood relative. Norma Davis herself was on death's door, recovering from a triple bypass surgery.

Police determined that Jeri had been in Davis' house the Sunday before the murder and that she wore a pair of Nike shoes.

Jeri stated that she did come to Davis' house but only came to drop off groceries. She heard the TV on upstairs but did not go up to say hello. She left the groceries on the counter and went home.

Police questioned why she didn't say hello but after weeks of questioning police determined that Jeri was not a suspect. She instead became an ally to the investigation.

CAPTURE

Descriptions obtained from the various merchants at the shopping center were eventually used to catch Dana. She had been buying so much stuff that the credit card company called June Roberts' family to inquire about the excessive spending.

Police detectives went to all of the stores where Roberts' credit card had been used, interviewing the cashiers. They obtained a physical description of Dana, surmising that the killer had dyed her hair recently and was accompanied by a little boy.

Detective Greco relayed this information to Jeri Armbrust.

Jeri surmised that the killer was in fact, her step-daughter Dana. She said that Dana recently dyed her hair red and had a boyfriend who had a young son.

Greco then obtained a search warrant and called for the aid of ARCNET (Allied Riverside County Narcotics Enforcement Team) to stake out Gray's home in Lake Elsinore.

Unfortunately, Dana was murdering Dora Beebe just hours before they determined her to be the killer. They followed Dana to a bank where she used Beebe's credit card and then went out for another shopping spree.

"We were able to follow the paper trail created by the use of these credit cards," Greco said. "With the merchants we were able to get a general description of the suspect."

Later that day, Greco arrested Dana while she was cooking dinner. Assisting officers took her boyfriend and his son in for questioning.

HOUSE OF STOLEN GOODS

Police did a thorough search of Dana's home after her arrest.

"They found jewelry, food, liquor, a ski mask, a purse with nearly $2,000 stuck in the washing machine, and many items of clothing," one report stated. "The police obtained a wealth of evidence: Gray's use of credit cards, clerks who had seen her directly after each murder, handwriting experts who identified her signatures on various items."

Dana was interrogated for hours.

"In the interview," Greco recalled. "Dana talked about finding a purse. And that purse belonged to a woman by the name of Dora Beebe. I knew that I had the right suspect in this case. But I didn't not know that on the same day we were serving her search warrant she was killing her last victim."

Dana stated that she never took the credit cards but after police revealed that they had evidence of her using them, Dana claimed that she found both Roberts' and Beebe's cards.

She maintained this story throughout the questioning. When asked why she kept the cards she said that she "had an overwhelming need to shop."

NO REMORSE, NO SYMPATHY

Dana displayed no sympathy for the victims. One psychologist noted that some of Dana's answers were like a robot answering in a manner they believed a normal human should.

After a hearing, Deputy District Attorney Richard Bentley wanted the death penalty. Dana pleaded insanity for all charges. But a witness came forward and stated that she saw Dana at Roberts' house on the day of her death, Dana quickly changed her plea to guilty and robbing and murdering two women as well as the attempted murder at the antique shop.

"At the end of the day," Dixon said. "Dana didn't want to die. When a witness came forward and said she saw Dana at the Roberts' house perhaps she knew that she was done for and would have been executed. Maybe she did not have enough confidence in her ability to pull off the insanity defense. So she struck a deal. She would plead guilty and avoid the death penalty."

Nonetheless, prosecutors were still unable to determine how Dana left the bloody crime scenes without a speck of blood on her or any sign of a struggle. All the clerks and waitresses spotted nothing out of the usual.

LIFE WITHOUT PAROLE

On October 16th, 1998, Dana Sue Gray was sentenced to life without parole.

"It's hard to find words to describe the atrocity in this case," Judge Patrick Magers said during Dana's sentencing. "The crimes were horrendous, callous and despicable."

Dana is currently jailed at the California Women's Prison in Chowchilla.

"She enjoyed the power," Dixon said. "She got addicted to the power she obtained while she killed people who were helpless to fight back. She liked watching them struggle. Liked having control over them before they died."

Jail has not seemed to bother Dana as she referred to her incarceration as her "county condo." She continues to pester her jailers to replicate her high-maintenance civilian lifestyle. She insists on a vegetarian diet and wants the use of a chiropractor. She has requested a mirror and has lobbied consistently for the return of her belongings.

Dana has drawn chilling clown faces, cobbling her paints together from M&M's candy coating, cherry drink mix, lipstick and and baby powder.

Her family came to visit her and brought her a pair of cheap Nike's. She refused them, wanting the high-end models.

Dana continues to thumb her nose at authorities as she sometimes sends collectibles to "murderablia" websites. She has sold her panties at $250, where she autographs them and writes in her prison identification number. She sells her hand tracing for $65 and a 'prison worn shirt', decorated with a drawing of a blue butterfly perched on a skeleton's hand.

"We can look back and say that she was simply psychotic," Dixon said. "And it is really easy to dismiss her killings as someone who was simply crazy violent and not read into it anymore than that. But in looking at the ages and gender of the victim, we can see the connection.

All of her victims were old enough to be her mother. So perhaps in Dana's mind she saw her victims as substitutes for her late mother with whom had a lot of anger toward. And I mean violent, aggressive anger. So when she subdued her victims with the phone cord, she would unleash a torrent of rage, smashing them with irons, stabbing them with utility knives,bashing them over the head with wine bottles. She would attack them and have flashbacks of her battles with her Mom, doing things to the victim that she was powerless to do to her mother as a little girl."

"She was doing it all for Mommy."

HELL'S BELLE : THE TRUE STORY OF BELLE GUNNESS

104

LINDSAY GARRETT

A serial killer is defined as a person who commits murders three or more times. Serial killing usually takes place because of an abnormal and perverted psychological gratification. As for the murder, they can take place over the course of more than a month. There is usually a significant break between two murders, this break being called a cooling off period. However, some agencies like the FBI tend to disregard the criterion of three murders. For them, even two murders can be classified as serial killing. Usually, the serial killer acts alone. Psychological gratification is the typical motive behind serial killing but it is not the only motive. Attention seeking, anger and financial gain are other possible motives.

Throughout history, there have been a number of serial killers who acts have horrified their fellow men. The names of some such as Jack the Ripper have achieved notoriety. They have been called monsters and worse. Nonetheless, the fact remains that all of them took the lives of other human beings no matter what their reasons were.

Belle Sorenson Gunness was one who fell into this category. She was Norwegian-American and stood six feet tall and weighed more than 200 pounds. No wonder, she was rather physically strong. She ended up killing most of her boyfriends and suitors. Horrifically, she also murdered two of her daughters. It is not verified but seems very likely that she killed her two husbands and all her children on varying occasions. Her motives apparently seem to have been to collect life insurance, valuables and cash. Elimination of witnesses was another possible motive. According to reports, she has been responsible for the murders of at least 25 people over the course of several decades. Some reports claim she murdered 40.

This is the biography of a ruthless woman whose abominable deeds earned her nicknames such as Lady Bluebeard, Hell's Belle and the Mistress of Murder Farm. She has gone down in history as one of the most prolific serial killers of America. What is surprising is that her crimes were not discovered before 1908 by which time, she had already fled leaving behind a farm full of dead bodies.

1. The Early Years of Belle Sorenson Gunness

The origins of one of the most notorious female American serial killers are rather murky and debatable. The majority of the biographers of Belle Sorenson Gunness have stated that she was born on the 11th of November, 1859. Her birthplace is believed to be somewhere around the lake of Selbu in the county of Sør-Trøndelag, Norway.

Belle Sorenson Gunness was christened as Brynhild Paulsdatter Størset. She was born to Paul Pedersen Størset who worked as a stonemason and his wife Berit Olsdatter. Her parents had 8 children of which she was the youngest. The family lived at a rather small cotter's farm called Størsetgjerdet located in Innbygda. Innbygda itself lies 60km away from Trondheim in a southeast direction. Trondheim is the largest city in the central region of Norway and it lies inside the Trøndelag county.

An Irish TV documentary told of a story about the early life of Belle Sorenson Gunness. Although the story is a rather common one, it has remained unverified by experts so far. As per the story, the event took place in 1877. Belle was attending a country dance even though she was pregnant. At the dance, she was attacked by a man who ended up kicking her abdomen. This caused Belle to end up miscarrying her child. As the man came from a rich family, he escaped being prosecuted by the authorities in Norway. The event changed the personality of Belle significantly according to people who knew Belle. An interesting thing to note about this story is that the man died soon after this event. The death of the man was said to have been caused by stomach cancer.

Whether this story is true or not is still up for debate. However, the fact remains that she immigrated to the United States of America. Since Belle had grown up poor and in poverty, she took service on a bigger and wealthy farm. She continued working there for 3 years so that she could accumulate enough money to pay for her fare for her trip to USA. She seems to have been emulating the example of one of her sisters, Nellie Larson. Larson had immigrated to the country earlier.

In 1881, Belle came to the United States of America. She adopted her new name as it seemed more American. In the beginning, Belle found work as a servant.

1. The First Victim

The thing about serial killers or even a murderer is that it is not easy to predict one. It is not always possible to identify a killer until the first murder. So far, with Belle, there has been nothing in her life to suggest that she would be capable of killing more than 25 people. However, things began to change from the year 1884.

In 1884, Belle wed Mads Ditlev Anton Sorenson in the city of Chicago, Illinois. 2 years later, the couple opened up a confectionery store. Unfortunately, the business did not become a success. Within just one year, the store burned down rather mysteriously. It was not too bad for the couple as they managed to collect the insurance. This insurance was used to pay for another home.

Some researchers believe that the couple did not have any children. However, there are investigators who have reported that Belle and Mads Sorenson had four children. They were Caroline, Axel, Myrtle and Lucy. Out of these four, Axel and Caroline died in their infancy. It has been alleged that acute colitis was responsible for their deaths. The symptoms of acute colitis include fever, diarrhea and nausea, cramping and lower abdominal pain. However, these symptoms are also displayed by a variety of poisoning. The lives of Axel and Caroline were supposedly insured. The insurance company apparently paid out.

Sorenson also had two life insurance policies to his name. On the 30th of July 1900, Sorenson was found dead. What is remarkable is that the 30th of July was also the only day on which both policies overlapped.

The first doctor who checked Sorenson believed that he had died due to strychnine poisoning. This was not the view of the family doctor of the Sorensons'. The family doctor had been treating Mads Sorenson for an enlarged heart condition. It was the belief of the family doctor that the cause of death was heart failure. Since the death did not seem to be suspicious by anyone, an autopsy was not performed. As for Belle, she told the doctor that she had only given the medicinal powders to her husband so as to make him feel better.

The very next day after the funeral of Mads Sorenson, his widow, Belle went to the insurance companies to apply for the insurance money. The relatives of Sorenson believed and even claimed that Sorenson had been poisoned by Belle so that she could collect the insurance money.

According to the surviving records, an inquest on Sorenson was ordered. However, there are no records to show whether the investigation actually went ahead. It is also not clear if the body of Sorenson was ever exhumed for the purposes of detecting arsenic as per the demands of his relatives.

Belle, on the other hand, managed to collect around $8,500 from the insurance companies. That amount would be equivalent to approximately $240,000 in 2012. Belle used the company to buy a farm located on the outskirts of the city of La Porte in the state of Indiana.

On the 13th of June, Belle and her family was included in the United States Census in the city of Chicago. As per the census, Belle was recorded as the mother of 4 children out of whom only 2 were living. They were Myrtle and Lucy, then 3 and 1 years old. The census also mentions an adopted girl of 10 years. She was identified as possibly being Morgan Couch. However, it seems that she was apparently called Jennie Olsen later.

It seems very likely that Belle Sorenson killed her husband for the sake of money. However, there is no proof about it. Whether she killed her two children or not is also up for debate. Even if she did, she got away with it.

1. The First Murder Suspicion

Belle Sorenson moved to La Porte in Indiana in 1901. She bought a house on McClung Road. According to reports, it seems that the carriage and the boat houses were burnt down completely within a short period of time after Belle had bought the property.

More important is what happened as Belle Sorenson was moving to La Porte from Chicago. During her move, she became acquainted with Peter Gunness. Peter was not only born in Norway but he was also a recent widower. They decided to get married and the ceremony took place on the 1st of April, 1902.

Just one week after the wedding, the infant daughter of Peter Gunness died. The cause of death remained uncertain but it was known that she was alone in the house with Belle. Again, it has remained unclear whether Belle was responsible for her death even though it does seem very likely.

Peter Gunness himself met his death in December 1902 in what was called a tragic death. Apparently, Peter was trying to reach for his slippers which was located close to the kitchen stove. It was at that moment when he got scalded with brine. This was the report by Belle Gunness after Peter's death. However, Belle later claimed that it was actually a part of a grinding machine for sausages that fell on Peter's head from a high shelf. The part caused a head injury that turned fatal.

Belle Gunness managed to get $3,000 out of the death of her husband but some sources claim that the amount was around $4,000. Be that as it may, the people of the locality did not believe that Peter Gunness could have been so clumsy so as to die in such a way. He was known in the locality to be a hog butcher with considerable experience. Additionally, Peter had been running a hog farm in the La Porte property. The district coroner was called to review the case. He unequivocally announced the fact that Peter had been murdered. A coroner's jury was also convened by the district coroner in order to look into the case.

Even though the situation looked bleak, Belle Gunness managed to somehow successfully convince the investigators and jury that she was completely innocent and that she had got nothing to do with her husband's death.

What is interesting is that Belle Gunness made no mention of her pregnancy at the time. She was already carrying Peter's son who was born in May 1903. The son was named Philip. By revealing her pregnancy, sympathy might have been inspired but Gunness did not do so for some reason.

Approximately a year after Peter's death, his brother, Gust came to take away his older daughter. The girl, called Swanhild, was taken away to Wisconsin. As such, she became the only child to have survived being with Belle Gunness.

For the next few years after Peter's death, Belle maintained a low profile. Keep in mind that she may have already been responsible for the deaths of two husbands and three children. According to psychology, it is not easy for a serial killer to give up their ways. Belle Gunness, the serial killer, would soon return and she did.

Her next murder took place in 1906. Late that year, Belle informed her neighbors that Jennie Olsen, her foster daughter, had joined a Lutheran College located in Los Angeles. However, some of her neighbors were told that Jennie had joined a finishing school meant for young ladies. In reality, Jennie was murdered by Belle. Her body would be found buried in the La Porte property later.

Belle continued to run her La Porte farm from 1903 to 1906. Another turning point in her life came in 1907 when she employed Ray Lamphere as her only farm hand to help her with the chores at the farm. Ray Lamphere would go on to play an important role in her story.

1. The Years of the Suitors

In 1907, Belle Gunness, as she was known after her marriage to Peter Gunness, hired a man called Ray Lamphere to work as a farmhand at her farm. However, this was not the only major decision she took during this time. Her other decision would have far reaching consequences and certainly paved her way to becoming a full-fledged serial killers.

Belle Gunness began to place advertisements in the matrimonial columns in newspapers to attract men who would later go on to become her victims. She chose not only the daily newspapers of Chicago but also the daily newspapers of other major cities in the Midwest.

The advertisement mentioned the following points. A beautiful widow with a large farm in La Porte, Indiana, wants to make the acquaintance of a gentleman. The gentleman should be well provided as the widow wants to join fortunes. The gentleman should be willing to come for a personal visit.

On hindsight, there are quite a few points about the advertisement that stands out such as the need for wealth and a personal visit. Suffice to say, quite a number of men responded to the advertisement placed by Belle Gunness. Of course, they were men of means as well.

One of the men who appeared at Gunness' farm was John Moe. He had come from Elbow Lake in Minnesota. He arrived with over $1,000. The purpose of the money was to help Gunness pay off the mortgage according to what he told the neighbors. Gunness introduced John Moe as her cousin to the neighbors. In just a week of his coming to the farm, John Moe disappeared.

Another of these suitors was George Anderson. He hailed from Tarkio in Missouri. He was also an immigrant from Norway. During dinner, Gunness broached the subject of her mortgage with Anderson. Anderson was willing to pay for the mortgage but only if they ended up getting married. That night, Anderson was sleeping in the guest room. He woke suddenly only to find Belle Gunness standing over him and peering into Anderson's eyes while holding a candle. The expression on Gunness' face was murderous and highly sinister. Anderson was so shocked that he yelled loudly. That seemed to have surprised Gunness who proceeded to run away from the room immediately without saying a single word.

Anderson felt very uncomfortable and terrified. He seemed to have guessed at the intentions of murder that Gunness had. As such, he got up from the bed and got dressed. He then fled Gunness' house without even saying goodbye. Even as he was running away, he still kept one eye over his shoulder. He was afraid that Gunness would come after him. Once he reached the station in La Porte, he took the first train going to Missouri. He did not bother to come back for his belongings or speak to Belle again. Anderson remains to be the only suitor to have escaped the LaPorte Black Widow.

Anderson wasn't the last of Gunness' suitors however. There was Ole B. Budsberg from Iola in Wisconsin. He was an elderly widower. The last time he was seen alive was on the 6th of April, 1907 at the La Porte Savings Bank. There, Budsberg mortgaged his land in Wisconsin and signed a deed. He got several thousand dollars in cash as a result of the transaction. Oscar and Mathew Budsberg, his sons, did not even know that Ole Budsberg had gone to visit Belle Gunness. Once they learned of his destination, the sons contacted Gunness. Belle replied promptly and stated that she had never seen Ole Budsberg.

Throughout 1907, many middle-aged men came to Gunness' farm. They seemingly appeared for brief visits and then disappeared. One of her last visitors was Andrew Helgelien. Helgelien was a bachelor farmer with whom Gunness started corresponding some time in December 1907. He came from Aberdeen, South Dakota. Previous to his arrival, Helgelien had exchanged many letters with Belle Gunness. Her last letter to him is what prompted his arrival. Helgelien seems to have been overwhelmed with the contents of the letter. It was dated 13th of January, 1908 and was found later at the Helgelien farm.

The letter ended with the words, 'Come prepared to stay forever'. In hindsight, that sentence seemed to have come true.

Helgelien visited Gunness in January, 1908 as the response to the letter. Helgelien carried with him a check for the sum of $2,900, which was his savings that had been drawn from Helgelien's local bank. A few days after his arrival, Helgelien and Guinness were seen at the Savings Bank, La Porte, where he deposited the check.

Helgelien disappeared a few days later after that event. On the other hand, Gunness visited the Savings Bank twice to make deposits of $500 and $700. It was also during this time that Belle Gunness began to have problems with Ray Lamphere, her farm hand.

In March 1908, Belle Gunness began to correspond with Lon Townsend who worked as a horse dealer and farmer in the city of Topeka in Kansas. Several letters were exchanged between them. He had been invited to visit her but he decided to wait till spring before he visited. By the time he was ready to visit, there was a fire at the Gunness farm. As such he could not visit. Another person who escaped this face was a man from the state of Arkansas. He, too, had to cancel his visit due to the fire. Another person was Bert Albert. Allegedly, Gunness had promised to marry him. However, the marriage was called off as Bert Albert did not have much wealth.

There was certainly no shortage of suitors. However, none of them, being as lucky as Anderson, left the farm of Belle Gunness alive. By the time of Anderson, Gunness had started to order huge trunks. These trunks were to be delivered to Gunness' home. Clyde Sturgis, a hack driver, was responsible for many of these deliveries from La Porte. Later, Sturgis remarked as to how Gunness was capable of lifting up those huge trunks as if they were 'boxes of marshmallows' and tossed them over her shoulders and took them inside the house herself. This goes on to show how strong Gunness was.

It was noticed that Belle kept the shutters of the house closed irrespective of whether it was day or night. Belle kept mostly to herself. Additionally, farmers who travelled by the farm at night often noticed her digging around in the hog pen with a shovel.

1. The Story of Ray Lamphere

Ray Lamphere was hired by Belle Gunness to work in her farm as a farmhand. However, Lamphere fell in love with Gunness deeply. In fact, he was willing to perform any chore for Gunness irrespective of how dirty or gruesome the task was.

With all the men visiting Belle Gunness for her hand in marriage, Ray Lamphere began to become very jealous of them. He began to cause scenes with Gunness. On the 3rd of February 1908, Gunness fired Lamphere from his job. Within a short period of time from that date, Gunness visited the courthouse of La Porte County and presented herself. There, she declared that Ray Lamphere, her former employee, had lost his mind. As such, he was a menace and danger to the public.

Somehow, Belle Gunness managed to convince the local authorities for holding a sanity hearing for Ray Lamphere. Of course, Lamphere was found and declared to be sane and, therefore, released. A few days later, Gunness visited the sheriff. She complained that Lamphere was visiting her at the farm and arguing. She mentioned that he seemed to pose a threat to her family. As such, Lamphere was arrested on the charges of trespassing.

That did not stop Lamphere from returning to the farm again and again. However, Gunness managed to drive him away. Lamphere even began to make threats, thinly disguised though. In one particular instance, Lamphere had confided to William Slater, a farmer, that Helgelian would not bother him any more as they had 'fixed him for keeps'. By that time, it was believed that Helgelian had vanished from La Porte a long time ago.

On the other hand, the brother of Andrew Helgelian, Asle Helgelian, became disturbed and concerned when Andrew did not come back home. He wrote to Gunness and asked if she knew anything about the whereabouts of his brother. Belle replied that Andrew was not at her farm. She also mentioned that Andrew might have possibly gone to Norway to visit his relatives. This did not sit well with Asle who said that he could not believe that Andrew would do such a thing. More importantly, Asle believed that Andrew was still somewhere in the vicinity of La Porte. It was, after all, the last place that Andrew had been seen and heard. Belle Gunness decided to brazen it out. She wrote back to Asle informing that he could come and search for his brother if he wanted. She would even help him conduct a search. However, Gunness also cautioned him saying that a search for missing people was an expensive task. As such, Asle should be ready to pay for Gunness' efforts if she had to get involved in the search. Asle Helgelian would certainly come to La Porte but that visit would take place in May 1908. By then, things had changed.

In the meantime, Lamphere became a danger to Belle Gunness. Additionally, Asle Helgelian seemed to be making inquiries which could end with her being sent to the gallows. Belle Gunness realized that something had to be done.

Belle contacted M.E. Leliter, a lawyer in the city of La Porte. She told him that she was afraid for her life as well as that of her children. She stated that Ray Lamphere had threatened to kill her and even burn down her house. Belle wanted the lawyer to create a will just in case Ray Lamphere managed to carry out his threats. The later did comply with the wishes of Gunness and drew up the will. According to the will, the entire estate of Gunness would be left to her children.

After concluding her business at the lawyer's office, Belle Gunness visited one of the banks in La Porte that held that mortgage for her property. She paid off the mortgage. However, Belle Gunness failed to visit the police and inform them about the threats to her life by Belle Gunness. It was only later that it was realized that she had intentionally not visited the police. After all, there had never been any threats from Ray Lamphere. All of the talk at the lawyer's office was mere ruse and the setting up of an elaborate plan that would come into effect only later.

1. The Fire at the Gunness Farm

In the wee hours of 28th April, 1908, Joe Maxson woke to the smell of smoke in his room. Joe had been hired as a replacement for Ray Lamphere back in February 1908. That morning, he was sleeping in his room on the second floor of the house belonging to Belle Gunness.

On that morning, Joe opened the door to the hall only to find it engulfed in flames. He screamed out the names of Belle Gunness as well as that of her children. However, he did not get any response. He shut the door and decided to jump out from the window of his room on the second story in just his underwear. He barely survived the fire which had by that time nearly covered the entire house. Maxson ran to the town in order to get help. Unfortunately, by the time the old fashioned fire truck arrived at the farm, it was already dawn and the house was nothing more than a pile of smoldering ruins.

In the midst of the ruins, four bodies were found. One of the bodies belonged to a woman. It could not be immediately confirmed if that body belonged to Belle Gunness as the head was missing. In fact, the head was never found. The 3 other bodies belonged to the children of Belle and they were in their beds when found. Was this the tragic end of Belle Gunness? Not quite.

County Sheriff Smutzer had come to hear about the alleged threats given by Ray Lamphere somehow. After taking one look at the scene in the farm, he decided to hunt for the farmhand. The lawyer, Leliter, also came forward and told about his meeting with Belle Gunness. He mentioned how Gunness was afraid that Lamphere had threatened her. He told that Gunness had mentioned among the threats that Lamphere would also burn her house down.

As things stood, the future seemed bleak for Lamphere and he did not do much to improve his cause. When Sheriff Smutzer found him, Lamphere was reported to have asked if Gunness and her family got out all right. What is surprising is that he asked the question even before the sheriff said anything. Only then was he informed of the fire.

However, Lamphere denied having any connection with the affair. He claimed that he was not present when the conflagration erupted. This proved to be false when a youth called John Solyem came forward. John claimed that he had been near the house and that he saw Ray coming down the road moments before the fire. Lamphere alleged that the boy was lying. However, Solyem claimed that Lamphere had found him hiding behind the bushes and that he was threatened by Ray.

1. The Investigation and the Discovery

The headless woman proved to be a source of consternation for the residents of La Porte. It did not seem to be the body of Belle Gunness after all. A neighboring farmer of Gunness, C. Christofferson declared that the remains were not that of Gunness. L. Nicholson, a farmer, and Mrs. Austin Cutler, also said the same thing. Some old friends of Gunness from Chicago, Mr. Sigward Olsen and Mrs. May Olander examined the body and said that it did not belong to Gunness.

The remains were then measured by doctors. After making allowances for the missing head and neck, they found out that the corpse could only belong to a woman with a height of 5 feet three inches and a maximum weight of 150 pounds. Neighbors and friends were fairly certain that it could not have been Gunness. Measurements were also taken from the stores where Gunness bought her clothes.

A comparison between the two sets of measurements proved that the body could not belong to Belle Gunness. Another crucial fact came to light by Dr. J. Meyers who examined the corpse's internal organs. He discovered that the organs contained strychnine in lethal doses.

It was during this juncture that Asle Helgelien made his appearance in La Porte. He informed Sheriff Smutzer about his suspicions that Gunness was responsible for the disappearance of his brother. However, it was the statement of Joe Maxson that spurred the Sheriff into action. Maxson informed the Sheriff that he had to carry loads of dust into a big area that was meant for feeding the hogs. That area was fenced by high wire and contained a number of deep depressions. The holes were covered by dirt and Gunness had said that they contained rubbish.

With this information, Sheriff Smutzer had to take a few men to the farm and start digging. On the 3rd of May 1908, the first body was unearthed. It was discovered to be the body of Jennie Olson who had vanished in December 1906. It was followed by the corpses of two unidentified children. Later, Andrew Helgelien's body was unearthed. More and more bodies began to be discovered.

1. The Aftermath

On the 22nd of May 1908, Ray Lamphere was arrested on the charges of murder and arson and tried. He denied these charges. However, the subsequent investigation found him guilty of arson. However, he was acquitted of murder as the body was proved not to be that of Belle Gunness. He was sentenced to serve 20 years at the State Prison on the 26th of November, 1908. On the 30th of December, 1909, Lamphere died of tuberculosis.

On the 14th of January, 1910, the clergyman, Rev. E.A. Schell, assigned to comfort the dying Lamphere came forward with an astonishing confession. In the confession, Lamphere admitted to the crimes of Gunness and also swore that the woman was still alive. Before his death, he confessed to the reverend as well as to Harry Meyers, a fellow convict, that he had never murdered any person. However, he did mention that he had helped Belle Gunness bury her victims. He mentioned how Gunness went about her killings.

Lamphere's confession also cleared up the mystery of the headless corpse found in the Gunness home. According to his statement, the woman was lured from Chicago by Gunness under the pretension of offering her a job as a housekeeper. The woman was decapitated and dressed to look like Gunness. As for the children, they were smothered to death.

After setting the house on fire, Gunness was supposed to have met Lamphere. However, she betrayed him and left via the open fields instead of meeting him at the road. By Lamphere's account, Gunness had murdered 42 men and taken money from them. By the end of her career, she had accumulated more than $250,000 which would be $6.3 million in 2012.

At the end, the true fate of Belle Sorenson Gunness remains a mystery. As it happens with such cases, people have claimed having seen her over the years none of which could be confirmed. On the

5th of November, 2007, the headless body was unearthed in order to determine once and for all if it actually belonged to Belle Gunness with the help of DNA analysis. However, there was a lack of DNA to compare it to. As such, the mystery of her end continues.

1. The List of Victims at the Gunness Farm

There were many bodies found at the farm owned by Belle Gunness. In fact, there were so many bodies that a sluice had to be created to separate the bodies from the dirt.

Positive Identifications:

- Ole B. Budsberg
- Henry Gurholdt
- Thomas Lindboe
- John Moe
- Olaf Svenherud
- Olaf Svenherud

Possible Victims

These are plausible victims who may or may not have met their demise at the hands of Belle Sorenson Gunness.

Herman Konitzer

William Mingay

George Berry

Christie Hilkven

Charles Edman

John H. McJunkin

Chares Neiburg

Henry Bizge

Tonnes Peterson Lien

T.J. Tie

CAROL SUMNER

DINA LIVINGSTONE

When James "Reggie" and Carol Sumner moved to Jacksonville, Florida for their retirement, they had visions of good health and happiness. They never thought that their overnight invitation to long-time South Carolina neighbor, Tiffany Cole, would end up the way it did; With the Sumner couple being buried alive.

Reggie and Carol Sumner were high school sweethearts in North Charleston, South Carolina. They were the kind of couple that everyone envied as they walked down the hall. Unfortunately, their lives pulled them in different directions. Reggie decided to serve his country in the navy. After finishing his tour, he got married and landed a job with the railroad. Carol also married and became a devoted mother, however, her first marriage ended in divorce, and her second nearly killed her. In 1987, after years of abuse, her husband at the time shot her seven times in their home before driving away and turning the gun on himself. Her daughter, Rhonda Alford, just ten years old at that time, spent almost a year helping her mother recover from her wounds. She had to help her bathe, dress, and take care of the house. After taking eight years to fully recover, Carol went back to work as soon as she was able. For over twenty-five years she was a civil servant at the Citadel and the Charleston Air Force Base. She also worked a second job at night at a Belk department store, among other jobs she would take when needed. She did whatever she had to in order to make ends meet. Shortly after her recovery, she found out that the blood transfusion she had received during her previous trauma had given her Hepatitis C. She was angry because she felt as though she could not escape her late ex-husband, but she refused to let it ruin her life.

She soon started a new job at a cable company and it was during this time that her life finally changed for the better. Nearly forty years after they'd left high school, a chance encounter brought Carol and Reggie together again. One night in 2000, a phone call was made to the cable company where Carol was working, which she received. After talking with the customer Carol and learning his name, she realized that he also sounded just like the Reggie she remembered. So she asked him if he was the same Reggie Sumner who attended Garrett High school in South Charleston. It was. They decided that they should get together after not seeing each other in so long. This time, though they were inseparable. Like "teenagers in love", a quick courtship led to love and then marriage in 2001 with a ceremony at Carol's home in West Ashley. Carol's daughter has said of Reggie "he was just a very gentle, kind and giving spirit. You could not ask for a better friend, husband or stepfather." Eventually, after retiring, the couple decided to move from South Carolina to Jacksonville, Florida. Reggie had previously bought a house during his days working for CSX railroad and as he was a "brittle" diabetic in frail health, he thought he would be more comfortable in the warmer climate. Carol agreed. "She only went down there to honor her husband," Rhonda said. Before moving, they decided to sell their Chevrolet Lumina to the stepdaughter of a friend who lived down the street, Tiffany Cole. They allowed her to make payments on the car to help her out and she agreed, often driving down to Jacksonville with friends to make those payments. Tiffany and the Sumners became friends and Tiffany would often spend the night at their house when she and her friends went down south. A pleasant girl on the outside, the Sumners had no idea what Tiffany could really be like.

Tiffany Ann Cole was born on December 3, 1981, to her sixteen-year-old mother, Shirley Duncan. Her biological father was in jail. She had no male role model to look up to or who could offer her protection the way a father should. Her mother had a boyfriend, but he was beyond cruel and especially loved to torment Tiffany. At one point, she had a puppy which her stepdad threw against a wall, breaking its neck right in front of her. He was abusive verbally as well as physically and Tiffany claims that as a young girl, he began to molest her, beginning around age eight. As a young teenager, she turned to alcohol and drugs to deal with the pain. In high school, Tiffany was a student who participated in cheerleading and played the flute. She was also a girl scout member but eventually the alcohol and drugs took over her life and she quit her programs and dropped out of school. At one point she fell in love with a boy with severe epilepsy, who ended up breaking her heart and since the only example of love from a man came from an abusive stepfather, this breakup reinforced the belief that she should expect to be treated badly and let down by men. She began looking for love in all the wrong places. In May of 2005, during a six-month period of prostitution, Tiffany ran into a man by the name of Michael Jackson. They were drawn to each other right away and began to get high and sleep together.

Michael James Jackson, born May 12, 1982, had a significant criminal history beginning in childhood. Born to a drug-addicted mother, he was mostly raised by his grandmother. He had multiple felony convictions but only for things like fraud and theft. After meeting Tiffany and becoming close, they took a road trip, first going to Myrtle Beach, then driving to Jacksonville, Florida, where they would be staying with Michael's best friend, Alan Wade. Born May 22, 1987, Alan and Michael had known each other for just over a year. When Tiffany and Michael arrived in Florida, they stayed at Alan's mom's house. After just a few days, though, she kicked them out because she was tired of the loud noises and constant partying. With nowhere else to go and with all their money spent on the nights of drinking and partying, Tiffany remembered that the Sumners lived nearby. The three friends showed up at their doorstep and explained what had happened. The couple was very happy to see Tiffany and invited her and her friends to stay the night. While they were chatting and catching up, Carol mentioned how worried they had been about their house in North Carolina not selling. There was no need to worry, however, because not only did their property sell, but they had also made a $99,000 profit. It was this general statement to a long-time neighbor that sealed the Sumner's fate.

It's difficult to know just whose idea it was to rob the Sumner's. Some say it was both Tiffany and Michael, while others say it was Michael who was the plan maker and master manipulator. Either way, a plan was hatched to rob and kill the loving couple. At some point in June, Alan had contacted his friend, Bruce Nixon Jr., and told him of a plan to rob someone. No other details were given. Then on July 6th, Alan called Bruce, born May 9th, 1987, and asked him if he would be interested in joining the others in digging a hole. Bruce agreed and stole four shovels from his neighborhood. The other three friends drove to Bruce's house in a rented Mazda RX-8 that Tiffany had rented in

South Carolina. The group drove around hoping to find a perfectly remote place for the hole to be dug. Alan asked Bruce if he knew of any good places to which Bruce responded that he did. He took them into Georgia, to a wooded area just over the state line. Leaving the car parked on the road, the group walked through the wooded area into a clearing where they began to dig a hole while Tiffany held a flashlight. It was approximately four feet deep and six feet square. Upon completion of the hole, they left the shovels and went back to the car. It was here that Alan asked Michael if Bruce could join in on their robbery plan. Michael agreed. The foursome drove back to Alan's house but his mother would not allow Michael in as she believed him to be a bad influence on her son. Over the next couple of days, it was Tiffany's job to remain in contact with Carol and Reggie in order to gain information from them about their plans and whereabouts. The foursome also secretly watched the house in order to figure out the Sumner's routine. It was unclear yet as to whether or not the group would enter the home while the couple was gone or if they would simply go in with the couple there. It was ultimately decided that they would enter the home while the couple was there so that they could get their financial information and the means to access their accounts. Michael said that he would kill the victims by injecting them with a lethal dose of their medications. He then promised that the four friends would split the money they received from the Sumner's accounts, each receiving about $50,000. They began making preparations for their plan. Just after midnight on July 8th, 2005, Michael, Tiffany, and Alan went to Wal-Mart and purchased disposable rubber gloves. On the evening of the murders, they went to an Office Depot, where Tiffany bought duct tape and a large roll of plastic wrap. Last, they bought a toy gun that shot plastic pellets.

Around 10pm., on July 8th, 2005, Tiffany drove the other three group members to the Sumner's house in the Mazda. Herself and Michael remained in the car while Alan and Bruce went up to the door. They had the duct tape and toy gun and both were wearing the plastic gloves. After Carol answered the door, Bruce and Alan told her that they were having car trouble and asked if they could use their phone. Carol said of course they could and invited them in. As soon as the boys entered the home, Alan pulled the phone cord out of the wall. Bruce pointed the gun at the couple. Alan grabbed Reggie around the neck and pushed him down into a chair. They told the couple that they wanted credit and debit cards and any other financial information. Carol began pleading with the boys not to hurt them. Bruce took the couple into a spare bedroom where he used duct tape to bind their legs and hands and to cover their mouths and eyes. Alan sent a text message to Michael, informing him that everything was under control. Michael then also entered the home and he and Alan began searching for financial information. They saw a pile of mail and financial statements which they put into a plastic bag. They spotted Reggie's prized coin collection and took that too. Michael told the other two to take the couple into the garage at which point they put them into the trunk of the Lincoln Town car. Tiffany went into the house and grabbed some of their belongings, put them into a bag and took the bag with her to the Mazda. Following the plan, both cars headed towards the gravesite, stopping only once to put gas in the Lincoln. Upon arrival at the site, Michael opened the trunk and apparently began screaming when he saw that the duct tape had become loose and the couple had worked the tape off. It had been over 100 degrees in the trunk. Sweat had caused the tape to loosen. They had also taken the tape off their eyes and were huddled together. Michael ordered Bruce to tape them up again, which he did. Alan then attempted to back up the car to the edge of the grave but, unable to do so, Bruce took over. Michael then sent Bruce up the road to wait with Tiffany at the Mazda. While still alive, the Sumners were taken out of the trunk and pushed into the hole. It is unclear as to who actually did the burying because Alan and Michael each blamed the other. Somehow, Michael ended up getting the personal identification number of the Sumner's bank account. Reports differ on whether he obtained this information from somewhere in the house or if Carol told him the number while being threatened to be buried alive. According to one documentary, Carol had gotten the tape off her mouth again when in the hole. Michael was telling them that if they didn't give up their PIN, they would die, at which point Carol yelled it out. It didn't seem to matter either way though because they continued to shovel dirt onto the scared couple.

After filling the hole, Alan and Michael put the shovels back into the trunk of the Lincoln and drove it up the road to where Tiffany and Bruce were waiting with the Mazda. The four of them drove to Sanderson, Florida, where they abandoned the Lincoln after wiping it clean of fingerprints. They then drove back to Jacksonville where they immediately went to an ATM and withdrew money from the Sumner's account, before retiring to a hotel. Alan and

Tiffany went to another Wal-Mart where they purchased more latex gloves as well as bleach. They returned to the Sumner's home in order to clean up any evidence. They also stole a computer. Bruce stayed with the group for another day and then went home, but Alan remained with Michael and Tiffany who returned to South Carolina, where Tiffany rented two hotel rooms; one for herself and Michael and one for Alan. It should be noted that after returning home, Bruce went to a party with a plastic bag filled with different medications. At one point he announced that he had found a new job murdering people. He stated that he had buried people alive and killed them without mentioning the involvement of anyone else.

On the morning of July 10th, Carol's daughter, Rhonda, decided to report to police the fact that she hadn't been able to get hold of her mother for a few days. Since they kept in touch on a regular basis and spoke every couple days, it was highly unusual for her mother to not return her calls. The next day, the Jacksonville Sheriff's Office (JSO) went to the Sumner's home. The back door of the house was unlocked and in the kitchen there dirty after-dinner plates, which was also highly unusual for the couple. The JSO began to investigate the financial accounts of the couple and they found that large amounts of money had been withdrawn within a short time frame. Video footage from the ATM machines that the group had used showed Michael's face and the silver Mazda in the background. On July 12th, after Rhonda made a plea on local TV networks for the safe return of her parents, the Sheriff's office received a phone call from someone posing as Reggie Sumner.

Dispatch contacted Detective David Meacham of the Sheriff's office and put the caller through.

Meacham: Where are you at?

Michael: We're in Delaware right now

Meacham: And what city is that in?

Michael: It's in Corpus

Meacham: Corpus, Delaware?

Michael: Yes

However, the town of Corpus, Delaware does not exist. Next, Tiffany came on the phone posing as Carol.

Meacham: Is this Carol?

Tiffany: Yes, sir, it is.

Meacham: Okay. This is Detective Meacham from the Sheriff's office. How are you doing tonight?

Tiffany: I was sleeping

Meacham: I understand. I understand you have some health problems

Tiffany: Mmhmm

Meacham: Okay. Any other problems?

Tiffany: I'm really tired right now

Meacham: What kind of problems do you have?

Tiffany: Cancer

Meacham: Cancer?

Tiffany: Mmhmm

The detective called Rhonda into the station so that she could listen to the taped conversation. She confirmed that the people posing as the Sumners were definitely not Carol and Reggie. The main reason for the call was to ensure everyone that the Sumners were alive and well and because the bank accounts had been frozen. They asked the detectives to reinstate the accounts, which they did so that they could track the money in order to locate the perpetrators. They also had the phone number from which Michael had called. Using this information, they were able to find that the phone was registered to Michael and that a call had been placed to a car rental agency in Charleston. They also learned that the cell had been used near the Sumner's home the night of the murders. Detective Meacham contacted the rental company and was told that the car had been rented to a Tiffany Cole and that it was overdue. Using the rental car's GPS system, they were able to find that the car had also been near the Sumner's residence during the time of the abduction. Using the cell phone trace, the car's GPS and the photos of Michael at different ATMs, police were able to locate the general whereabouts of the three murderers. On July 14th, with help from Tiffany's brother, who was on probation and threatened with jail, police raided a Best Western hotel in Charleston and arrested Tiffany Cole, Alan Wade, and Michael Jackson. Bruce Nixon was also picked up at his home in Florida.

While Tiffany, Michael, and Alan refused to cooperate with law enforcement, Bruce appeared to have some semblance of a conscience because he broke down and admitted to the crimes right away. He also agreed to lead police to the burial site. For the first time in TV history, documentary footage showed Bruce and detectives at the grave site where Bruce broke down in sobs. Excavation of the site began the next day. The victims were found fully clothed in a crouching position. Reggie had somehow broken his tape and was holding Carol's hand. There was two feet of dirt over their heads. With ten years of homicide under his belt, Detective Meacham said it was one of the saddest and most horrible things he had ever seen. The medical examiner determined that both Reggie and Carol were alive in the hole before they were buried. Their nostrils, mouths, throats, esophagi, and trachea had fine sprays of dirt in them, which indicated that they had inhaled it. They died from mechanical asphyxiation and smothering, caused by the dirt covering their heads while compressing their chests. She said it was the worst case of asphyxiation she'd ever seen. It was "horrendous."

At some point while in jail, but unaware that Bruce had come clean, Michael's grandmother called him.

Grandma: Michael, listen to me and don't say a word. You're in the newspaper. All over the newspaper yesterday and today

Michael: For what?

Grandma: Murder

Michael: What?!

Grandma: Murder. 'Bodies ID'd as former South Carolina couple James and Carol Sumner. Bail was denied for 18-year-old Bruce Nixon of Florida who was arrested and charged with murder, home invasion, robbery, and kidnapping.' He took them to the grave site and everything

Michael: Oh my God. Are you kidding me?

Grandma: It's right here in today's paper

Michael: Bruce took them to the f*****g spot. The f****r showed them where the spot was at?

Grandma: Yes, dear

Michael: *starts panting* Bruce just killed us all

Bruce Nixon told detectives everything that had happened and agreed to testify on behalf of the prosecution. He wasn't sentenced until after he testified against the other three group members, but in the end, he received 45 years for each victim, currently being served concurrently at Century Correctional Institution in Florida. Alan Wade was tried first.

Michael Jackson was the first to be tried. Testifying on his own behalf, Michael stated that the plan was only to rob the Sumners and that it was not going to involve murder. He said that Alan and Bruce went into the house and when they came out they drove off in the Lincoln which he then followed. He claims he had no idea that Reggie and Carol were in the trunk. According to Michael, when they arrived at the hole in Georgia, it was Alan and Bruce who told him where to park and to bring them a flashlight. It was when he arrived at the burial site that he heard Carol moan. He then stated that he questioned what the other two were doing before returning to the Mazda to wait. He did admit to impersonating Reggie. Bruce testified that Michael had been the ringleader and was the one who orchestrated everything. After stepping down from the witness stand, Carol's daughter, Rhonda, said of Bruce, "I just wanted to hug him. He is a murderer, but in the end, he did the right thing." It was that testimony that she believed sealed Michael's fate because he was found guilty of first degree murder, robbery, and kid-napping, and sentenced to death for each murder. He is currently on death row in Florida.

Alan was next to be tried. Two witnesses who were not identified gave victim impact statements during the penalty phase. Alan's lawyer then called six of their own witnesses to testify including Bruce Nixon, Alan's mom and sister, the mother of a friend, his middle school principal, and his youth pastor. Overall, the witnesses testified that Alan's parents divorced when he was eight and his father disappeared from his life. His mother took him to church regularly and as a kid, he was kind, smart, and well-behaved. After the divorce, his mother was unable to spend a lot of time with him because she had to work a lot to support them. When he was in his teens, his mother had a bout with breast cancer. By his early teens, he began to use drugs. In the sixth grade, he was involuntarily committed to a 72-hour hold because of a drug related incident. When he was sixteen, his mom had to take him out of school or be arrested for his truancy. The next year, his mother kicked him out of the house in an attempt at tough love because his drug use was becoming worse. In 2004 Alan introduced her to Michael, whom she immediately saw as a bad influence on him. Since his arrest and before his trial, Alan had apparently become a model prisoner, obtained his G.E.D and tutored other inmates in math. Nothing seemed to sway the jury, however, because he was found guilty on all counts and voted eleven-to-one to receive the death penalty. He is also currently on death row in Florida.

Tiffany was the last to be tried. Her lawyer argued that she wasn't a major participant in the crimes. He said that she was under the control of her boyfriend Michael, and that he was the mastermind. Tiffany claimed that she believed the crime would only constitute a simple theft and that she didn't knowingly participate in the robberies, kidnapping or murders. She insisted that she did not know that Reggie and Carol were in the trunk of the Lincoln until they arrived at the burial site. The circuit judge, Michael Weatherby did not see it that way, stating that it was she who held the flashlight during the digging of the grave and was there when they were bound and placed in the trunk. He also noted that she was the one who purchased the duct tape and gloves and later pawned the jewelry and computer they had stolen. "She was thoroughly involved," Weatherby stated. "She knew exactly what she was doing and participated without hesitation." It was noted as well that she was the only one of the four who had previously known the Sumners. During the penalty phase, the prosecution called two of the victim's family members who gave impact statements. The defense attorney then called up witnesses who testified that Tiffany was of good character. Three of those witnesses were correctional officers who stated that Tiffany had been no trouble in jail and did not cause any problems. A psychiatrist, Dr. Earnest Miller, testified that she suffered from poly-substance and alcohol abuse, chronic depression, and a personality disorder. He also stated that she had witnessed abuse to family members and had been sexually abused herself by her stepfather. On the other hand, he testified that Tiffany was competent and thus he could not support a plea of insanity. Finally, he stated that she knew right from wrong and had a high average IQ. In the end, Tiffany was also found guilty of all charges and sentenced to death by a 9-3 vote. Upon hearing her fate, she bowed her head and turned to her mother, mouthing the words "I love you". Her lawyer, Quentin Till, said she had been ready for the decision. He visited her in jail that week. "I told her to be strong," he said. "...I still see her being utilized and manipulated by Michael Jackson." Revis Sumner, Reggie's brother, said that Tiffany has since written to the family, asking for forgiveness. He says he has forgiven her, but that doesn't mean she shouldn't suffer for her actions. The Reverend Jean Clark, Reggie's sister has said, "I pray for Tiffany. I pray for all of them. I'm grieved that these four young people have wasted their lives." Chief Assistant State Attorney, Jay Plotkin, who tried all four cases said, "All of these defendants got exactly what they deserved. Justice was done." After the sentences were given and the trials were over, Reggie's son, Frederick Hallock, said, "You expect some sort of closure or some sort of good feeling when the verdict is read, but it didn't seem to help much. I just know they didn't deserve this." Currently, Tiffany is one of only five women on Florida's death row. At the time of her sentence, she was the sole woman there.

Tiffany, Michael, and Alan all filed appeals after their trials, citing multiple issues. All three were denied and their sentences were upheld. Recently, in 2015, Tiffany filed another appeal, asking for a new trial. She claims that her defense lawyers were ineffective and that she should not have been convicted of first-degree murder since she did not actually bury the bodies herself. But according to Florida law, it doesn't matter who actually committed the murder. Just knowing that it was going to happen is enough to warrant a guilty verdict. At her original trial Tiffany said, "But please remember I didn't do this. I am not the monster that created this, but I regret meeting him," referring to Michael. Upon hearing that Tiffany was asking for a new trial, Reggie's sister, Jean had this to say: "Most people are going to try to come back with something like that after the fact, because they're going to try to find a loophole and get off. But justice has a voice, and justice has to be served." And the thought of going through another trial breaks her heart. "I have family members that are still not the same and never will be the same. In fact, I don't like to involve them too much into things like this, because they can't deal with it."

In 2014, Alan Wade also filed an appeal for a new trial, citing that his lawyers did not do a good job of representing him. His appellate lawyers said that his original defense lawyers barely met with him before the trial and didn't interview witnesses prior to putting them on the stand. They also cited the lack of objections to supposedly questionable evidence. In December 2014, it was decided by the Supreme Court of Florida that his conviction be upheld.

Previous to that, Michael Jackson filed an appeal for a new trial, stating that his lawyers were also ineffective. As with Alan's trial, Michael claims that his lawyers did not make objections to certain evidence when there was clearly an objection to be made. The judge did allow an appeal hearing for his concerns and at the close of the hearing, Michael was allowed to make a statement. It went as follows:

First, I'd like to say that I am guilty of the crimes of first-degree murder, kidnapping, and robbery against Mr. and Mrs. Sumner. My reason for wanting to address the Court today is because of the many lies I told to everyone years ago at pretrial and then trial. I downplayed my involvement to look as if I were not guilty but the truth is that—the truth is that it was my idea to do this. Truly, I did not make anyone do anything. All were willing participants but I was, in fact, the leader. It was my idea to do it. I lied to this Court all throughout my trial testimony, same to [defense counsel and the State]. Even more so I lied to the people who deserve the truth the most, the family of Mr. and Mrs. Sumner, and for that, I am deeply sorry. There are no words that I could ever offer that would convey the depth of my remorse or sorrow, but again I say that I am truly sorry for what I have done and though I'm undeserving, I do ask forgiveness. My desire today is to reconcile the truth to the family of Mr. and Mrs. Sumner and to Your Honor, the attorneys and to the Court record. If necessary, I will answer any and all questions fully and truthfully. Thank you.

His conviction was upheld. Tiffany, Michael, Alan, and Bruce remain in jail today, with the former three on death row.

"It's sad," said Rhonda Alford about her parents. "It took them so long to find each other." Carol and Reggie's ashes sit in an urn in Rhonda's home, forever mixed and blended together.

DRUG CRAZED KILLER : THE TRUE STORY OF ROSIE ALFARO

ELIZABETH MARKS

Maria del Rosio Alfaro, better known to the media a Rosie Alfaro, is the first woman to be sentenced to death in Orange County. Her story is a tragic one, set in a town nearby Disneyland in Anaheim, California. By the time that Rosie was thirteen, she was heavily into drugs and considered by many to be an addict. At this age, Rosie was often doing fifty speedballs a day for weeks at a time, a speedball being a mixture of heroin and cocaine. Regular doses of this highly addictive cocktail were just the first steps along a dark path, and in grade seven she dropped out of school. By the time that Rosie was fourteen years old, she had become a prostitute. Despite efforts from her mother to get her back on track, a tormented and abused past pushed her forward on her path of self-destruction

At the witness stand in a court case only a few years after this point in her life, an old friend of Rosie's Tamara Benedict testified that at that time they both often slept with drug dealers for money so that they could buy drugs. Sometimes just receive their payment in narcotics directly. Benedict claimed "we had no jobs at all" and "sometimes we would steal from stores or get someone to steal for us." By the time that Rosie was fifteen, she was a single mother. At 18, she was a mother of two and pregnant with twins. It is also at this age that she committed the murder that would ruin her life.

When Rosie had been pregnant with her second child, she had spent some time living at the Wallace residence, the family of one of her friends from school. The Wallace's had three girls, Amber, April, and Autumn. Rosie was friends with April Wallace and was taking shelter at their house during one of the most difficult periods of her life. After her time living with the family, she got back into drugs, became distant, and had very little contact. The only time that she would have any association with the family would be when she was offered a lift somewhere.

A year later, when Rosie had had the baby and was pregnant with the twins, she was living with a relative of the father from her most recent pregnancy. This house was three blocks away from the Wallace residence. Rosie was on another drug binge at the time and had her first hit at eleven in the morning. By 2 PM she was getting desperate for another fix. She began to think about how she could acquire the money for more drugs. She mentioned to the men that she was with, the three of them looking after her oldest child, that she had an old video camera that she had left at the Wallace residence. She asked them to drive her to the residence so that she could retrieve it, and that she would gladly trade this camera in for cash so that they could all get another hit. The two men, Rosie, and her eldest boy who was only fourteen months old at the time drove to the Wallace residence. Rosie got out by herself to go and knock at the door, and the two men stood outside of the car with the baby. Rosie has made different testimonies in her time, both claiming that she didn't know that nine-year-old Autumn Wallace would be home and that she did realize. Whichever of these is true, Rosie knocked on the front door and Autumn answered. Based on her testimonies, it is more likely that she was expecting Autumn to be home so that somebody would enable her to get inside of the house.

Autumn's school had had an 'early day' that afternoon, and they had let the children leave at 2:35PM. Her mother wasn't due home from work until after five, and neither of her sisters were home. Rosie asked if she would be able to use their bathroom to fix her hair and freshen herself up. Autumn, who remembered Rosie from the time that she spent living with the family, didn't hesitate to let her in. Before Rosie had knocked at the door, Autumn had been cutting out paper dolls. She went back to her task in the living room. On her way to the bathroom, Rosie went to the kitchen and picked up a knife. In the bathroom, she created a ruse to trick Autumn. She claimed that she needed assistance with an eyelash curler, and asked Autumn to come into the bathroom to help her. When Autumn entered the bathroom, Rosie grabbed her. "That's when I did it," Alfaro told the investigators. "I stabbed her . . . 'cause she knew who I was," Rosie claims that Autumn made no sound when she was attacked and that nobody else was involved. "I was too high; I just remember her looking at me," Alfaro when she was interviewed at Orange County Jail. "Before, sometimes at night, the day would come back, and I'd block that out. Now I think about it more and more, because blocking is not working." Alfaro attacked Autumn with such ferocity that she died on the spot.

In all of Rosie's later testimonies, she claims that she was forced to stab the girl by one of the men who had accompanied her. She also claims that she stabbed Autumn several times, but that she did not finish the deed. Whether Rosie acted alone or with this man who she still refuses to identify, Autumn Wallace was stabbed fifty-seven times in her face, chest, and back. After this time, Rosie claims that she and the man went around the house stealing a few items. They took a portable TV, a typewriter, a telephone and a Nintendo set. Later on, they sold these items for a mere $300. As Rosie began to come down off her high, she realized the severity of the things that she had done and the guilt began to set in. She began to panic, and it was then that she made plans for her escape.

At 5:15 PM, April Wallace returned home. She found the door unlocked and the house in a mess. She called out to Autumn but got no response. She immediately ran to the house across the street for safety where she could wait for her mother to come home. Linda Wallace, the girls' mother, arrived home at 5:40 PM. She was told that her house had been burgled and that Autumn was missing. Believing that her girl might be hiding, she went inside the house to search for the youngest daughter and found her in the back bathroom in a pool of blood. Neighbors told Linda that they had seen a brownish Monte Carlo parked outside of the Wallace house and that two men were standing outside of the car. One of them was holding a small child. Police fingerprinted the house and found prints that matched Alfaro's. They brought Rosie in for questioning, and she denied any involvement in the murder, or that she has been near the house at all. As they didn't have any further evidence or a witness that could identify her having been at the house, Rosie was let go.

At some point after the murder, Rosie asked one of her friends if she could leave a bag full of clothing outside of their house. She had made plans to leave for Mexico the next day, and wanted this bag to be easily accessible. However, Rosie never showed up. Investigators found out about the bag and inside they found a pair of Alfaro's tennis shoes and a pair of April Wallace's boots stolen from the house. They put out a warrant of arrest for Alfaro, and brought her in for questioning again. It was at this point that Alfaro began to realize that she wouldn't get away with the crime, and that she would have to be more cooperative with the police.

Alfaro identified one of the men that she had been with as Antonio Reynoso, being the man who stayed in the car with her son. Antonio had been released from prison the previous day. He had agreed to share his drugs with Rosie is she was happy to share her needle. The other man, who Rosie claims was active in the killing of Autumn Wallace, she has persistently refused to identify over the years, and only refers to by the name of Beto. Alfaro has said several times in court that she is not able to identify this man for the police as she fears for the safety of her children and her partner. Even if the face of the death penalty, Rosie did not reveal the identity of this man, and he still remains a mystery. Some members of the court have claimed that they feel the story of Beto is a fabrication, and that Rosie committed the crime by herself. However, there is some evidence to suggest that her claims might be true. Not only did neighbors see the two men out the front of the house, but a footprint in the bathroom that was initially thought to belong to Rosie was found to not match the shoes that she had been wearing. While all of the prints had initially been assumed to be Alfaro's, criminologist Marc Taylor found that there was also another set of prints both inside and outside of the house. This gives some credibility to Alfaro's story, but her unwillingness to identify the man means that she is taking the full consequences for the situation alone. Alfaro claims that when Beto saw that Autumn was home, he became enraged and put a knife to Rosie's back. He threatened to stab her if she wasn't going to stab Autumn. Rosie admits to stabbing Autumn several times, but maintains that Beto was the one who did the majority of the stabbing and caused Autumn's death. "If I wasn't so scared my family would get hurt, I'd tell the truth, but I just can't," she said in court. Even though it means that she is potentially getting the death sentence for a crime that she didn't solely commit, she remains silent on this issue in order to protect her family.

As Rosie plans to die with the identity of Beto, it is likely that this person will never be brought to justice and remains at large. Rosie initially claimed that the man was a friend of her father's, and that his name was Miguel. Later she claimed that this was not true and that the man who she would only name as Beto had a woman's name tattooed on the side of his neck. Alfaro identified a photo of the man. Orange County investigator Robert Harper identified the likely identity of this man to be Robert Frias Gonzalez, but Rosie gave no confirmation of this suspicion. It was later revealed the that tattoo on the side of his man's neck was actually a butterfly, but due to Rosie's state of mind and drug abuse her claims have not been judged as entirely false. It is impossible to say whether Rosie was identifying a photograph just to appease the police, and that this explains the difference between the tattoos, whether she was in such a state of mind that she couldn't remember the tattoo correctly, or whether the man had any identifiable tattoos done over with larger and darker designs to hide what was underneath. The fact that there is a discrepancy between the tattoos certainly doesn't factor this final consideration. Perhaps if his tattoo was the name is a lost loved one, he marked it with a butterfly to keep his display of respect? A deputy sheriff at the Orange County jail testified that he had seen a man similar to the one that Rosie had identified in the picture getting into a blue Camaro outside of the Orange County jail. From the evidence, it would certainly seem that another person was present at the residence and may have had involvement in the murder of Autumn Wallace, but without Alfaro's testimony on this matter nothing more can be pursued.

In the courtroom Alfaro, wearing a floral blouse and blue stretch pants, cried throughout Tamara Benedict's testimony and also those of her childhood friends, her boyfriend Manuel Cueva, and her mother Silvia Melendez Alfaro. When Cueva described the visits of Alfaro's children to the County jail as Rosie awaited trial, she openly sobbed. Sylvia Alfaro made every attempt possible to try to create some sympathy and understanding for Rosie, painting an image of the horrific childhood that she had suffered through. Sylvia testified that her husband was a dreadful alcoholic who regularly hit her and Rosie in front of the other children in the family. He would also often throw the whole family out of the house when he was in a drunken rage. Alfaro's mother discussed Rosie's early drug use and how she seemed totally unable to quit her habits, constantly seeking to get some distance from the real world. When Rosie was pregnant with her first child at the age of fourteen, her father left home and abandoned the family. Sylvia claimed that Rosie completely lost control of her drug addiction at the age of fifteen. "She wore heavy makeup, black clothes and was always dirty. She didn't care how she looked." From this point until when Rosie attacked Autumn, she was in an almost constant state of pregnancy. With no other way to support her habit, she slept with her dealers and attempted to look after her children as best she could.

A mental health expert, Dr. Consuelo Edwards, was the first one that Rosie had told about Beto. It was Edwards that recommended that she should speak about Beto in court, and he also came forward to defend her with his testimony. From his interactions with Rosie, Edwards deemed that her intellectual functioning was 'borderline' and that he feels that she has a serious learning disability. He didn't argue that he felt this excused any of her behavior, but that it should be something to factor when the jury are arriving at their decision. He tested Rosie as having an IQ of 78, and testified that her intellectual issues were made worse by the traumatic experiences that she had gone through as a child. In reaction to these claims, the prosecutor called forth several employees at the Orange County jail who testified to Rosie's poor behavior in jail. These employees also claimed that they had heard Rosie saying "I'm a frustrated person who takes things out on people, and have to learn to live with that," and "I'm not going to be able to do this again. I'm no actor. I'm going to be cold this time. I just want to get this over with." It is not certain whether this was a move to try to paint Rosie as an inherently bad or disturbed person, as this claims as nothing to do with her capacity intellectually. Perhaps they were making the argument that Rosie's lack of intellectual giftedness mean that she wasn't able to reflect on her own behavior and that way that she treated others. However these testimonies were intended, they painted Rosie as incredibly difficult to deal with and as somebody who lashes out with quick and ill-thought-through responses.

The first jury that assessed the case was on 14th July 1992. The judge for this case claimed that her crime was the most "senseless, brutal, vicious, and callous killing" that he had ever known. The jury was a deadlock with 10:2 in favor of Rosie receiving the death penalty, meaning that this was not enough to hand down the sentence. A deadlock means that the required amounts of votes was not reached, and in order to place a person on Death Row every member of the jury needed to agree that this was the proper course of action according to the evidence that they had viewed during the case. When Rosie was reflecting on this outcome and how close she had come to being sentenced to death, she claimed that "I do think that someone has to pay for what happened to that poor little girl, and that's me," she said. "But I can't help thinking how my life stopped, ended, at 18, and that I have no future, and all that is because of drugs." In many ways, Alfaro has distanced herself not only from the person that she was when she committed the crime, but the person who engaged in the type of lifestyle that she did before that. As she awaited her next trial date, she claimed that she would spend all

day trying not to think about how likely it was
that she would be sentenced to death and instead
thought about the ways in which drugs had
wasted her life.

Then in 2007, another court hearing was held
where the jury placed forward the unanimous
decision for the death sentence. During this trial,
Rosie claimed that she was constantly haunted by
her actions. She read out a letter that she had
written to Autumn. "I have a picture of you in my
Bible, and every time I open it, I see your innocent
face and I think of my boys and what I would do
if something were ever to happen to them. . . .
So please know that I am deeply and truly sorry,
Autumn, and I will pay for the rest of my life
for what happened." Nobody can be sure whether
this was an attempt to show remorse and soften
the approach of the jury or whether Alfaro simply
felt the need to be able to express these feelings
in a more public context than she was capable
of in jail. Perhaps Alfaro wanted for the Wallace
family to hear that she was experiencing remorse
over the issue, and that she was making a genuine
attempt to comprehend and suffer for the things
that she had done. When the sentence was handed
down, Deputy Dist. Atty. Charles J. Middleton
described the jury's decision as "justified" and

claims that he knew the outcome based on the amount of time that the jury took considering the evidence, saying "I was sure it was a death verdict because I could not imagine 12 people agreeing that soon that this kind of a crime should not get a death sentence." These jury members deliberated for just over two days before they released their unanimous recommendation. When the sentence was handed down, it was met with clapping and cheering from the Wallace family and gasps and shock from the Alfaros and their supporters. Alfaro later claimed: "I know it's hard for the Wallaces to forgive me, and I don't ask for their forgiveness," Alfaro said. "If it had been one of my kids that was killed—I'm a mother too—I'd probably do the same thing: celebrate." William M. Monroe, who was Alfaro's attorney, quoted Alfaro as saying "I can't believe this. It can't happen to me.... Why did they (jurors) do this?" after the sentence was brought down. Monroe also made some emotional claims, seemingly unable to believe that Alfaro was truly going to be placed on Death Row. "I'm probably as shocked by the verdict as Rosie Alfaro is," Monroe said outside the courtroom. "I still contend that this crime was committed by a person with an abandoned and malignant heart, and Rosie Alfaro is not (such) a person." Monroe mentioned that "I feel terrible, absolutely terrible for what happened to Autumn Wallace, but this little girl, this young woman-child, does not deserve" and that he would file an appeal. After the verdict was served, photographers and cameramen were crowded around the courthouse hoping to catch a glimpse of the grief-ridden Alfaro. Alfaro supporters shielded their faces and turned their backs in an attempt to avoid the media. "Nobody wants to talk right now. We have no words," said a friend of the defendant. As with all cases, there was a lot of initial hype but it slowly died down. Now, when searching about the Alfaro case, there is rarely a recent article that will give any updates or further information on the matter. Rosie is simply on Death Row awaiting her visit to the gas chamber as her sons continue to grow up without her presence.

Much of the coverage around the case has regarded the behavior and quotes of the two mothers in the courtroom: Linda Wallace the mother of the deceased Autumn who claimed to fight for justice for her daughter's death, and Sylvia Alfaro who was fighting for the life of her own daughter. Linda Wallace made an emotional plea to the courtroom, claiming that during the trial her daughter has only been known as a young victim stabbed to death by somebody that she trusted. The grieving mother wanted everybody to know what Autumn was really like, and that was she so much more than the court case had reduced her to. She spoke about her blonde hair and brown eyes, and that she was an A student who loved swimming and fishing. She was incredibly creative, and wanted to be an artist when she grew up. Of Rosie, Linda claimed that what she did is horrible and that she will "never forgive or forget her." To Sylvia Alfaro, Linda said that she really felt for her because she knows what it feels like to lose a daughter.

Sylvia Alfaro was similarly trying to expand the way that the people in court were viewing her daughter, saying that "The first time that I came here, I felt like I was sitting in the electric chair," she cried. "I beg you, please forgive my daughter and please forgive what she did," Sylvia claimed that Rosie's issues with drugs had gotten a lot worse after the birth of her daughter's first son Daniel, and that she had enrolled her daughter in several drug programs in an attempt to beat her habits. Unfortunately, she always went back to her old ways after a few months. However, Sylvia maintains that while Rosie was pregnant she usually managed to control her drug addiction.

This does not align with the information that was presented before the court on the day of Autumn Wallace's murder. This particular binge might well have been an isolated event or even an extended period of drug usage, but in either case, it would have been difficult for the jury to believe that Rosie was not a drug user during pregnancies when the entire case revolved around her desperation for another hit. Sylia had even gone so far as to sent her daughter to Mexico to live with her grandmother in the hope that this distance and change of environment would help her to get away from the complicated lifestyle around drugs, but this change in location didn't make any difference. She ended up coming back home when her grandmother was not able to cope with her behavior, and she fell into the same patterns.

Monroe, the attorney, attempted to raise some sympathy for Rosie regarding her troubled past and attempted to make the case that she should be sent to prison instead of the gas chamber. He made this assertion based on her addiction to drugs and her being the mother of four young boys. He claimed that the jury made a mistake in their recommendation, and he also introduced the notion of race. Monroe claimed that the mainly white jury could not possibly understand what it was to grow up in a household like Rosie had, and that they could not "empathize, understand or relate" to Latino women trapped in the drug world. While it might be true that somebody in a very different demographic cannot fully understand the life of somebody who has endured so much pain, the purpose of a jury is to find a random sampling of people who can determine what they feel is just action and what behavior should be acceptable in our society. Regardless of Alfaro's abuse in her childhood and early teens, the murder of a nine-year-old girl is not something that the jury considered as acceptable behavior.

Linda Wallace and her daughters had been traveling from their new homes in Lake Havasu , Arizona, the girls both having married and started their own families. April Nunez and Amber Szabo had been traveling in support of their deceased sister and trying to come to terms with her loss. In one interview, their mother Linda claimed that "You would think after all this time, you would get over it, but you don't." When asked how she endured through a trial, two penalty hearings, and a fifteen-year wait for the appellate review, Linda claimed that "I was doing it for Autumn." Later she also claimed that "it's the only thing I can do for her," the mom said, "I need to be there to represent her because she can't do it. I go to be with my daughter." Linda Wallace has also confided in several interviews how she feels outside of the court. "The hardest thing for me is to see people now who are Autumn's age," she said. "Not being able to see her grow up, that's what bothers me the most. She would be 26 years old now. She could be married. She could have kids. That's what I think about." Linda says that she has spent the years waiting for justice, and not spending her time or energy thinking about Alfaro. "I know she is in a bad place," Wallace says. "I know she will never see the light of day. I am fine with it." Linda also commented that Alfaro hasn't had much of a life since her arrest: "she just exists," the mother said. "It wouldn't be any life I would want." While the Wallace mother was one of the members of the family who was clapping when the sentence was passed down and has also been somebody to proclaim often and loudly that her daughter needs justice, she has also stated that she doesn't feel the need for Alfaro to be executed. In some ways, this might be an attempt to show a soft side to the media as in many of her interviews she claims that she waited fifteen years for the sentence to be handed down, when Alfaro had been imprisoned for that entire duration. This suggests that, in some way, Linda Wallace did feel that it was necessary for Rosie to be put on Death Row to properly avenge Autumn's death.

April and Amber have expressed similar long-lasting hatred of Rosie. "We get nothing," Zabo said. "And she gets all of these things. It makes me mad. ... I just want to see her be put to death, and I want to see it faster than it is taking." When April was asked if she would travel to San Quentin Prison to watch Alfaro get executed, she said "Oh yes, I would go to watch her die, without a doubt. I would do it myself if they'd let me." Linda Wallace was also asked in the same interview, she responded "I am not that much for that," she said. "If she is put to death, then another mother loses her child. I know what it feels like to lose a child." But her other interactions with the media suggest that Rosie getting the death penalty gave her some sense of relief and faith in the system.

The judge, Middleton, claimed that Monroe did not give any credence to Monroe's claims of racial misconception, and asserted that the jury had made their decision purely based on facts. He went on to say that she made her own choices in life and that Rosie cannot blame her action on others no matter how poor her treatment as a child and young adult had been. He also put forward the opinion that based on the evidence in court he did not believe that Rosie Alfaro was capable of looking after her children. Alfaro was convicted of first-degree murder with special circumstances, the circumstances being that the murder offered during the felonies of Burglary and Robbery. Alfaro joined two other women on Death Row, Maureen McDermott and Cynthia Lynn Coffman. McDermott was a Los Angeles registered nurse who was convicted in 1990 of hiring a co-worker to murder her roommate. It was found that Maureen planned to collect on a $100 00 mortgage insurance policy. Coffman was convicted in 1986 of the kidnapping and murder of a woman in San Bernardino. Capital punishment was restored in California in 1978, and these are the only three women to receive the death penalty in that time.

Since she was handed down the death sentence, Alfaro says that she spends her time thinking about how misguided her drug addled youth was, what happened to Autumn, and the days when her children will be old enough to know what she did. "God, I hate to think of the future, because there's not a future for me and my kids," she said.

"It's going to be up to (them) if they still want to call me mom when they find out. I know they're going to find out sooner or later, and I'm scared of what they're going to decide." Alfaro is now 44 years old and still on Death Row with his four children still being cared for by boyfriend Cueva. She will not get to see them grow up, and may not feel that she deserves to give them any guidance in doing so. In many ways, she is now waiting for death as she no longer has a functional life. Waiting for the nightmare to be over do that she no longer has to block out the deeds of her past.

fland

Olaf Jensen
    Bert Chase
    John E. Hunter
    Emil Tell
    Lindner Nikkelsen
    Frank Riedinger
    Benjamin Carling
    Ole Oleson
    Aug. Gunderson
    Johann Sorensen
    Andrew Anderson
    And others

KILLER NIECE: THE TRUE STORY OF VERNICE BALLENGER

MARY EASTON

In 1983, Vernice Ballenger, with the help of her estranged husband Mac Ballenger and two other men, arranged the robbery and subsequent murder of her elderly aunt Myrtle Ellis. Her motive was simple—money.

It all began earlier that year, when Myrtle Ellis was involved in a car accident. She was taken to the hospital, where a rather unusual discovery was made. Ellis had $60,000 in cash on her person. This large sum of cash made headlines. Local newspapers ran stories on the odd occurrence. These stories caught the eye of Ellis's niece, Vernice Ballenger.

Believing that the elderly Ellis likely still had the cash, Ballenger devised a plan to rob her aunt and get the money. She enlisted the help of her estranged husband Mac Ballenger, who hired two acquaintances to rob Ellis in her home. However, they were unable to get the money and instead resorted to violence, murdering Ellis and setting fire to her home.

The crime went unsolved for years, until the wife of one of the men involved went to the police.

This is the story she told...

Early Life

Vernice Ballenger (born Alston) was born to Verner F. Alston and Marguerete Raspbery Alston in Carthage, Mississippi in 1937. She was the second of two children as she had an older brother, R.V. Alston.

Ballenger's early years appear to have been unremarkable. She remained in Leake County Mississippi and married Mac Ballenger. The couple would three children—one boy and two girls. In 1970, Vernice's brother R.V. Alston died tragically at the age of 35.

"Vernice was on the plump side," journalist Mark Crist said. "She had a perpetual frown on her face and wore rainbow colored moo-moos around the house. She had red hair and had an intense stare that could intimidate. But her bark was worse than her bite as she was on the cowardly side when push came to shove."

Mac and Vernice eventually separated. Mac moved to Greenville, Mississippi while Vernice remained in Leake County. They did not formally divorce however, and remained legally married, with Vernice keeping the last name Ballenger.

"There wasn't much doing in Leake County," Crist said. "The typical weekend for a woman was to go to the hair salon on Saturday and church on Sunday. That was Vernice's life and she didn't seem to want any more than that. Until she read about her aunt Myrtle."

Crime

Aunt Myrtle Involved in Car Accident

In 1983, Vernice Ballenger happened to read in the newspaper that her elderly aunt, Myrtle Ellis, was involved in a car accident. Ellis was injured, but her wounds were not life-threatening. She was taken to the hospital, where nurses discovered something odd—Ellis had $60,000 (roughly $145,000 in 2016 when adjusted for inflation) in cash with her at the time of the accident. The reason why is unclear, but the story was strange enough that it made the local newspapers along with reports of the car wreck.

While some may have argued that broadcasting the fact that this elderly woman, who lived alone in the country, had such a large sum of cash, could threaten Ellis's safety, it was done regardless. This oversight by local reporters proved to be fatal for Myrtle Ellis.

"It seemed hare-brained at the time to broadcast the fact that she had so much money," Crist said. "It really gives you an idea of how hard-up that small town of Carthage, Mississippi was for news. It was a small, rural town with one main street. Nothing happens there. But when an elderly woman is in a car accident has a lot of cash on here, that makes the news. It also invited an opportunist in Vernice Ballenger."

When Vernice Ballenger read about her aunt's accident and the large sum of cash she had on her at the time, her interest was piqued. Ballenger went to visit her aunt, intending to find out what she had done with her money since the car accident.

"Myrtle Ellis was a nice, sweet elderly woman," Crist said. "She lived alone out in the country. She spent her days sewing dolls and drinking tea. Didn't have a care in the world and would have no reason to suspect her own niece of coming over to steal her money."

Feigning concern for her aunt's safety, Ballenger asked about the money. Ellis informed her that she had put the hospital had taken the money and put it into a bank account for Ellis, where it was safely stored at that time.

"Vernice probably gave little thought as to how her aunt Myrtle came up with that kind of money," Crist said. "She just wanted it and would do anything to get it."

Despite Ellis's assurances that the money was now in the bank, Ballenger still believed her aunt had the money in the house or on her person somewhere. Far from being the concerned niece she pretended to be, Ballenger was in fact plotting to rob Ellis and take the money.

"Her aunt was telling the truth," Crist said. "But Vernice was so focused on getting some money that she completely ignored the fact that her aunt was telling the truth. That was the kind of mindset she had, once she believed one thing, in this case the idea that her aunt was still holding the money, she could not change her focus. Vernice lacked the silver-tongued harm of other female killers. She could not have manipulated her aunt into giving her the money. She would have to take it by force."

Planning the Crime

But Ballenger couldn't do it herself—after all, her aunt would recognize her. Instead, Ballenger sought the help of her husband, Mac Ballenger. Despite the fact that the couple was separated, Ballenger believed her estranged husband would be financially desperate enough to help her commit the crime. She drove to Mac's house in nearby Greenville, MS and asked him for assistance with the robbery. Mac refused, possibly believing that Ellis would recognize him as well, but told Ballenger he knew someone who would be willing to do it.

Mac enlisted the help an acquaintance of his, whom he believed would help commit the robbery, James Head. On July 9, 1983, Mac drove to Vernice's home in Leake County, where she lived with the couple's two daughters. Head arrived separately and brought a friend, Ronald Ritter, to help with the robbery.

"James Head was a local scumbag," Crist said. "The kind of guy who knows all the wrong people because he is 'wrong people'. Ritter was a huge guy. Muscular and intimidating with a beard and sleeveless shirts to show off his biceps. It took these two guys to rob an old lady."

The group met a second time at the Vernice's home the following morning, July 10, 1983. Here they would devise a plan for the robbery that ultimately led to the murder of Ballenger's aunt, Myrtle Ellis. Ballenger told Head and Ritter about the car accident and the $60,000 her aunt had had on her person at the time. She even told the men how Ellis had insisted she had since put the money in a bank account.

However, Vernice told her new co-conspirators that she did not believe her elderly aunt. She told Head and Ritter that Ellis likely still had the money somewhere in the house. She insisted that if Ellis did not give up the money, they should search the house. According to later testimony from Ronald Ritter, Balleger "said that she knew that [Ellis] had it, that if she didn't have it sewed in her brassiere, it would probably be inside of a chair, or something. She had a doll. It might be sewed up in the doll." Vernice encouraged the men to tear apart the house if Ellis did not give up the money willingly.

Vernice also agreed to give James Head and Ronald Ritter each $10,000 for their help with the crime, presumably thinking she could keep the other $40,000 of her aunt's money for herself and her husband, Mac. At this time, the three men and Ballenger had all agreed that they were only going to rob Ellis. According to all involved, they did not intend to hurt Ellis, and Vernice specifically told the men not to harm her aunt.

"Vernice knew her aunt's habits inside and out," Crist said. "She told them how the door was always open and exactly where she would be sitting when they entered the home. She gave them tips on how to terrorize the money out of her aunt but gave explicit instructions not to hurt her. Just to do enough to get the money from her."

Robbery Attempts

That same day, July 10, all four participants—Mac, Head, Ritter, and Vernice—drove to Ellis's house to scope it out and plan the crime. Ellis's house was located in a fairly isolated part of the country outside the more populated center of Leake County. The house was surrounded by a wooded area, making it even more isolated. The group returned together back to Ballenger's house to further discuss their plans before Head and Ritter would go back out to the house on their own to rob Ellis.

Head and Ritter drove to Ellis's house, intending to rob her and leave. However, as they drove through the woods and approached Ellis's home, they saw a hunter in the woods. Head and Ritter were frightened, believing they may have been spotted and that the hunter would later be able to identify them as the perpetrators of the planned robbery. The two men turned around and returned to Ballenger's home where Mac and Vernice were waiting.

When they returned and explained the situation to the Ballengers, Mac insisted that Head and Ritter were just scared. In order to loosen them up, Mac opened up a bottle of whiskey and the men began to drink. Head in particular drank rather heavily. The group discussed their plans further, agreeing once again that they would not harm Ellis, and Head and Ritter agreed to return to Ellis's house and go through with the robbery. This time, it was decided that Mac would go with them as well.

Before they left, Vernice Ballenger gave Head and Ritter a pistol and a rifle. Despite reassurances that they were not going to hurt the elderly Myrtle Ellis, the men took the guns with them. Curiously, Mac made no mention of the guns in his later confession to the police and statements in court, despite admitting to all other aspects of the crime.

Mac, Head, and Ritter made another trip to Ellis's house. By this time, the men had been drinking quite a bit. When they arrived at Ellis's house, Head and Ritter entered the house. Head had the pistol with him. Mac stayed outside, waiting on the porch for the other two men to come back out with the money.

Upon entering the house, Head and Ritter found Ellis and demanded that she give them the money. Ellis told the men she did not have any money in the house. She repeated what she had told to her niece, Vernice, telling the men that the money was not in the bank.

Head and Ritter became angry—Head, according to Mac and Ritter, was a large man and a violent drunk. Ritter first slapped Ellis, demanding that she tell him where the money was. Ellis became angry, insisting that she didn't have any money in the house. She told the robbers once again that the hospital had taken the money after her accident and put it into a bank account for her.

However, Head and Ritter either did not believe Ellis's story or were so infuriated by their failed robbery that they turned to violence. Head began hitting Ellis, knocking her unconscious. Even after Ellis lost consciousness, Head continued asking her questions, demanding to know where the money was. The later autopsy report revealed that Head beat Ellis severely, hitting her in the chest with a great degree of force.

Head pulled out the pistol, put it to Ellis's head and pulled the trigger, intending to kill her then and there. The gun was unloaded, however, and so Head began to beat Ellis with the gun, too. According to Ritter, Head went crazy, beating Ellis senselessly.

"We can't mitigate the perp's actions by blaming it on the alcohol," Crist said. "These men were pure scum. Slime balls of the highest order to beat and maul a defenseless old woman."

Convinced that the money was hidden somewhere on Ellis's person or in the house, Head and Ritter tore apart the house. Vernice had told the men the money was most likely sewn into Ellis's bra or a chair in the house. When Ellis's body was found later, her clothes were partially ripped, indicating that the men had perhaps searched her bra for the money as instructed by Ballenger. However, they were still unable to find the money, and eventually they gave up their search.

Meanwhile, outside the house, Mac searched Ellis's truck outside and found a doll, which Ballenger had also told the men might have the money sewn into it. Mac entered the house and told the men he had found the doll and believed it might contain the money. Head threw Ellis across the room and kicked her one last time, then the men left, leaving Ellis behind in the house.

All three men got back into their van, and Mac gave the doll to Head. Head tore the doll open, searching for the money, but found nothing. He threw the doll out the window and the men drove back to Ballenger's house.

Plotting the Murder

When the men returned to the house, Vernice asked them about the robbery. The men explained that they had been unable to find the money and told Ballenger what they had done. Ballenger was concerned. According to Ritter, she told the men that if Ellis had seen the van or seen Mac, she would know that Ballenger had been involved. Ritter stated that Vernice felt, "if [Ellis] seen Mac or anybody; she would know that Vernice was tied into it, so [we] couldn't leave the situation like that. Said we would have to kill the woman."

"Vernice did a total three-sixty," Crist said. "She realized that if her aunt had seen her vehicle outside the window that she would inform the police. So despite getting nothing out of the whole episode she ordered her 'hitmen' to go back and 'take care of' her aunt. Cold-hearted stuff."

She told the men they would have to burn down the house with Ellis in it in order to hide the evidence and avoid being caught. The group devised a new plan—Vernice Ballenger, Head, and Ritter would return to the house. They would drop Head off and he would start the fire. Then Ritter and Ballenger would return and pick up Head, then leave.

Ritter and Ballenger dropped off Head and drove down the road to wait. When they didn't see smoke coming from the house, Ballenger told Ritter that one of them would have to return to the house to make sure Head had started the fire. Ritter volunteered to be the one to return to the house and ensure it was burned down.

Ritter went back to Ellis's house to burn it down himself. According to his testimony later, Ritter planned to get Ellis out of the house before he burned it down, contrary to the group's original plan.

"While all of this was happening, Aunt Myrtle was dragging herself out of the house," Crist said. "So this was a remarkably tough woman with a strong constitution. She was beaten and bloodied. Her nose and mouth were bleeding. Her eyes swelling and she was having difficulty breathing. Despite all of that, she crawled out of her home and made her way outside. Somehow, someway, she had to get help. But she didn't find it fast enough. The men were on their way back."

Ritter found Ellis lying on the ground outside her home. He entered the house and found a pile of clothes on the floor. Ritter lit a match and threw it on the clothes, starting the fire.

"The men thought that Aunt Myrtle was already dead," Crist said. "If they thought she was still alive they would have most likely beat her to death or dragged her inside the house and set it on fire. Instead, they let her be."

Head, Ritter, and Ballenger all returned to Ballenger's house. Head and Ritter went back to Greenville, MS. Ballenger and Mac remained at Ballenger's home.

The fire department soon responded to the fire at Ellis's home. When they arrived, firefighters found the home burning. Ellis, however, had awoken at some point after the beating and dragged her badly beaten body outside. When firefighters and volunteers got to the scene, they found the now unconscious Ellis lying outside the house near a shed.

Although she had escaped the fire, Ellis was in bad shape and it was immediately clear she had been the victim of a brutal attack. Her head was swollen from the beating she had received at the hands of Head and Ritter and her clothes had been ripped. Ellis already had bruises forming on her body, and she was covered in dirt from dragging herself out of the house and through the yard.

"When the first responders arrived on scene," Crist said. "They immediately asked Myrtle if she knew who did this to her. She hesitated. She said that she knew who did it but did not want them to get into any more trouble than they already were. That was the kind of woman she was. She knew that it all led back to her niece, Vernice. She still played the role of a doting aunt even though she was beaten half to death."

Ellis's Death

Myrtle Ellis was transported to the hospital in Madden, MS, a nearby small town. Ellis remained unconscious the entire time she was in the hospital in Madden. Some time later, she was transferred to University Hospital in Jackson, MS to be treated by a neurologist.

While at University Hospital, Ellis briefly regained consciousness. She was questioned by police, who attempted to learn the identity of her attackers. However, Ellis once again refused to reveal the identity of the people who attacked her. Either out of fear or loyalty to her niece, Ellis never told the police what she knew. She survived for several days in the hospital, but ultimately succumbed to her injuries on July 20th, 1983 in University Hospital.

"She died a painful death," Crist said. "Miraculously, she survived for ten days after the beating as her entire chest cavity was smashed in. Unfortunately, she did not spill the beans on who did. It may seem like a forgiving act but the people involved looked at the prospect of getting away with the crime and possibly committing similar crimes in the future."

After Ellis died, an autopsy by William Featherson was performed to determine the cause of her death and search for any possible clues that would help police solve the crime. In the report, Featherson found that while there were some head injuries, including evidence of a possible hemorrhage in the brain, these injuries were not what killed Ellis.

Additionally, Featherson found extensive injuries in Ellis's chest area. These were likely due to the beating that Head gave Ellis, including throwing her across the room and kicking her. Ellis's four upper ribs on both her left and right side were fractured. Her breastbone was fractured as well, and her mammary artery, which runs alongside the breastbone, was torn.

This torn artery led to massive internal bleeding. Blood filled the right side of Ellis's chest, and according to Featherson, "collapsed her right lung and then pushed the heart and the left lung over into the left side of the chest cavity, and that, the hemorrhage and the displacement of the internal organs, is what produced her death." Featherson also said these injuries led him to believe she had been hit or kicked in the chest, and this attack caused her death.

Most damning of all, Featherson found no injuries caused by fire. This left investigators searching for the person, or people, who had brutally attacked this elderly woman in her home. But they found nothing. The only clue was the sighting of a van near Ellis's home around the time of the attack. This was, of course, Vernice's van. Police tracked down the van and Mac Ballenger confirmed that it belonged to his wife, Vernice Ballenger. However, Ballenger had since had the van painted and put new tires on. The trail of evidence went cold and it seemed Ellis's killers would never be brought to justice.

"The interrogation should have been a lot stronger," Crist said. "With some crack police work, they could have found out how Mac was connected to Ritter and Head. The police simply played their hand too early. They were investigators in a small town and really unused to this kind of brutality and conniving."

An Accidental Confession

Though it seemed for nearly a decade that this heinous crime would go unsolved forever, this turned out not to be the case. In fact, nine years later, the case was cracked wide open by one woman's slip of the tongue. In 1992, police went to the house where James Head lived with his wife. They were only there to serve civil papers entirely unrelated to the murder of Myrtle Ellis.

When they arrived at the home, Head's wife was present. She saw the uniformed police officers in her front yard approaching the house and immediately blurted out, "You're here about that murder my husband committed in 1983." This, according to Leake County prosecutor Mark Duncan, is what "got the ball rolling".

From this initial confession, police were able to arrest all four conspirators, including the mastermind behind this vicious crime, Vernice Ballenger. Mac Ballenger, James Head, and Ronald Ritter confessed to the crime, giving police the full story of how they had planned and executed this robbery gone wrong. Both Mac and Ritter also testified against Ballenger during her murder trial.

"Each of the men had pointed the finger at Vernice," Crist said. "There was no loyalty there. They would all get life sentences in the end."

Vernice Ballenger was found guilty of robbery and capital murder for her role in the killing of Ellis. In January of 1993, she was sentenced to death for her crime. Ballenger made several appeals, but her conviction was never overturned. Her accomplices were all sentenced to length prison terms, but only Ballenger was given the death penalty for her actions. Prosecutors stated that this harsh penalty would serve as a message to others in the area that crimes like Ballenger's would not be tolerated.

However, Ballenger was never given the death penalty. Instead, she died in prison of natural causes in 2002 at the age of 65.

"Vernice was fond dead in her prison cell," Crist said. "She lived out her last days alone and died alone. It was the epitome of a senseless act of violence that got her to where she was."

While it was not the punishment ordered by the court, Ballenger's death brought an end to the tragic case of Myrtle Ellis's murder.

MYRA HINDLEY

JACOB STILLMAN

In the early 1960s, Myra Hindley took her first job out of school at a small chemical company called Millwards Merchandise. A shy eighteen-year-old, she kept to herself, reading in the office courtyard during breaks.

But she only did this to attract her co-worker, Ian Brady.

Brady would spend his breaks reading books. Myra soon followed suit in the hopes that he would approach.

After several months, the Glasgow, Scotland native finally made his move.

They both worked at the office as clerks. Brady was four years older than her as they began to date.

Myra lived with her grandmother and gave her virginity to the awkward co-worker on her grandmother's sofa. She would soon become Brady's accomplice in some of the most gruesome child killings in the history of Great Britain.

A BAD NEWS CHARACTER

Brady already had a police record for petty theft. He also had a strange demeanor, tilting his head oddly at people as he stared them down with hooded eyes.

He was nicknamed "Lassie", not a reference to the Collie dog but to his feminine body language. Brady was tall, skinny and would indicate later that he was a bisexual. As a child, he had few friends and was called "Dracula" in the neighborhood. He would torture kittens and see how long it took for them to die.

They were both bookworms and Brady would give Myra books on the Marquis De Sade, trying to introduce her to the world of sexual sadism. After their dates, he would invite her back to his place and play back recordings of Adolph Hitler's speeches.

The young couple would come up with pet nicknames for each other. Myra would call Ian "Hetty" after a character in the Goons and he would call her "Hess" after Hitler's deputy. They would soon become inseparable, both strangely odd people that felt that were superior and set apart from everyone else.

It soon became clear, however, that Ian was influencing Myra and not the other way around. He was her guide to the world of sexual sadism and then later, slowly revealed his desire to rape and murder children.

He started this by sharing a book in the same way he introduced her to sadomasochism. The book had detailed the "crime of the century". A child was the victim and one of the characters was named Myra.

"He had given me a book called 'Compulsion,'" Myra recalled. "Which was the story of Leopold and Loeb. They decided to commit the perfect murder. They were studying the philosophy of Nietzsche, his theory of the superiority of the pure Aryan and the strong overcoming the weak. It was very much the Nazi philosophy. They kidnapped a twelve-year-old boy for a ransom. They killed him, were caught and sent to prison. I told him it was a very disturbing book. But why exactly had he wanted me to read it? He told me he wanted to do a perfect murder and I was going to help him. That was why he needed me to pick someone up as I was a woman and a child would be more trusting of a woman. I burst into tears and he slapped my head backward and forward. I managed to fight him off and told him to stop it."

Myra fell prey to Ian's system of push and pull psychology. He would be abusive to Myra then inexplicably turn around and be sweet to her.

"I must be totally honest and say he wasn't always cruel and sadistic towards me," Myra said. "We had some pleasant times in country places that he'd found during his travels on his bike. We'd pack a picnic lunch, lots of coffee, bottles of wine and spend whole days in peace and tranquility. That was such a contrast to the other side of him. These were moments I treasured and thought about when things were bad. Trying to remember, telling myself that he couldn't help what he was and maybe in time he would become accustomed to ordinary domesticity and we could live a normal life."

IDLE HANDS

"Myra was a bored English girl looking for some adventure," forensic psychologist Paula Orange said. "Brady had an edge about him. Myra liked that about him, she wanted out of her dull life and into a world of edgy darkness, if you will."

Myra didn't judge Brady for being an avowed Nazi. She thought he was just going through a phase but he continued to play Richard Wagner's music full blast and storm around the house dressed up in Nazi regalia. Working himself up into a frenzy, he would then play rough sex games with Myra.

Myra found this aspect of Brady's personality to be alluring. She enjoyed dressing up in leather and black stockings, indulging whatever fantasy Brady could come up with.

"She was a sheltered young woman," Orange said. "And Brady opened up a whole new world to her. Think of it as 'Fifty Shades of Grey' with some Nazism thrown in and you have the whole relationship of Myra Hindley and Ian Brady."

The kinky sex continued and Brady gave stronger indications that he wanted to commit the perfect murder.

He wanted to harm children.

But he needed an accomplice.

"We can make the case that Myra made the jump from sadomasochistic sex to murder out of an obligation to Ian," Orange said. "It gave her a rush, to follow his lead. She needed more and more to get that same high."

The two would feed off each other sexually after which Ian would begin to plot the murders out. Who would be their victim? How would they kill them? Where would they kill them? He wrote things out in advance to the most minute detail.

"She (Myra) became desperate to fulfill his fantasies, his needs," journalist Clint Entwhistle said. "She was frightened, I suspect, of rejection by him."

So Myra didn't report him. She went along with his program.

SNAPPED

Brady had made his decision that they were going to kill someone. The night before, he took Myra to a bar on the back of his motorcycle. The two parked a little beyond the pub itself. Ian then began to intimidate Myra. He was jealous that she took a ride home from a co-worker.

"All the time we were talking," Myra recalled. "He was running a knife across his fingers. I honestly thought he was going to stab me. Then he laughed, put the knife away, told me never to accept a lift (the co-worker) again, and we drove back to the pub."

"Later as we were driving home, I dreaded what he would do when we got there, for I knew he would do something. "He raped me anally, urinated inside me and, whilst doing so, began strangling me until I nearly passed out. Then he bit me on the cheekbone, just below my right eye, until my face began to bleed. I tried to fight him off strangling me and biting me, but the more I did, the more the pressure increased. Before he left, when he'd seen the state of my face, he told me to stay off work the next day ..."

This would all take place under the roof of Myra's grandmother who was asleep when the assault took place.

"My gran almost fainted when she saw me and went to get my mother, who asked me if ' He' had done that to me. My mother disliked him intensely and kept telling me he was no good for me; she'd been telling me that since I'd met him at 18 and a half, but what girl of that age listens to her mother when she is wholly infatuated and in love? I told them what he had told me to say (she had been hit by a beer bottle during a bar fight) but I knew they didn't believe me."

THE FIRST MURDER

The following night after he beat down Myra, Brady selected his first victim.

He spotted a teenage girl walking to a dance by herself. She wore a sky blue jacket over a button-down red polka dot dress. Her white gloves and high heels turned on Ian Brady but what really arrested his attention was her face.

Cute with an air of innocence. A face that had an easy vulnerability, someone who would crack under the pressure of his whip.

Her pain and tears would be delicious, Ian thought.

Her name was Pauline Reede.

Brady gave Ian her orders and told her to pick the girl up. He would follow them on his bike.

"Ian Brady was awkward," Entwistle said. "He was not the kind of person a child would trust. There is no way anyone would have gotten into a car with him."

That is what he needed Myra for.

Myra did as he said, driving up alongside Pauline as she walked on the deserted road. The two young woman had already known each other from around the neighborhood.

"Can I give you a lift?" Myra asked.

"Oh, thank you, sure," Polly got into the small white van.

"Where are you going?"

"To the dance hall-"

"Okay," Myra said. "I just have to go to the Moors. I just lost one of my gloves. You can help me look for it. It will only take a second."

Pauline simply nodded her head. She trusted Myra.

THE KILLING FIELDS

"The Moors above Manchester were a special place for Ian Brady and Myra Hindley," Entwistle said. "They picnicked there together. They'd have sex there. It was a very, very important place to them."

It would also be the place where they would commit their first murder together.

Myra stepped off the van and directed Polly to look through some bushes. It was dark and Pauline asked if they should just look for it in the morning. Myra laughed it off and walked away, feigning as if she were looking for her gloves.

Ian Brady waited in the bushes, his mouth dry with anticipation, as he watched the sixteen-year-old Polly sift through the bushes.

Sneaking behind his victim, he slammed her across the head with a shovel.

Pauline Reede fell to the ground, stunned.

She would then be raped, tortured then murdered by the sadistic Brady.

"Brady was a sadist," Orange said. "He got off on the suffering of his young victim. The more innocent she was, the more she screamed, the more she pleaded for her life, the more he got off. It was part of the high for him. He had moved beyond the bedroom thrills with Myra and needed a bigger high. He wanted his fantasy to become reality."

Brady assaulted Pauline until she lost consciousness.

No longer able to provide him the "fun" of listening to her suffer, he took a knife to her throat and killed her.

Myra watched in silence as Ian Brady commit the brutal crime and then proceeded to bury Polly in a shallow grave.

"He led me to her body which I tried not to look at," Myra wrote. "I didn't know at the time that he was testing me at there was no need for me to be there. He told me to look at here. I'll never be able to forget what I saw. I stood and looked at the dark outline of the rocks against the horizon of the dark sky. Three people died that night. Pauline. My soul. And God. No God would have let what had happened, happen."

On the surface, however, Myra didn't seem distressed about the murder. She went to work the following Monday as if nothing happened.

"You would think if she had any conscience left she would have gone to the authorities," Orange said. "But Myra had been dehumanized by that point. The daily rapes and assaults made her numb to everything."

Still, a part of her old self remained. The disappearance of Pauline Reade sent shockwaves throughout Manchester. Myra was reading the newspaper one day and noticed a personal column written by Pauline Reade's mother.

It read " Pauline, please come home. We're heartbroken for you."

"I began to cry," Myra recalled. "Rocking myself back and forth with the paper clutched to my chest. I didn't hear his bike, nor knew that he'd come into the house. He asked me what was wrong but I couldn't answer; I couldn't stop shaking and crying, for I was devastated about what had happened to Pauline, and for her mum and dad. I really liked Mrs. Reade and used to feel sorry for her because she had problems with her nerves and always looked as though she was on the edge of a breakdown. He grabbed the paper off me and soon saw what I'd seen."

"He put the bolt on the front door in case gran came back, did the same to the back door, and began to strangle me. Before I lost consciousness, I heard him remind me of what he'd said after Pauline's murder, and that threat still stood. After the first murder, as we were driving home, he told me that if I'd shown any signs of backing out, I would have finished up in the same grave as Pauline."

MYRA'S EARLY LIFE

As one would expect, Myra grew up in an abusive home.

Her parents engaged in daily shouting matches which she watched from behind her bedroom door.

Her father would routinely beat her mother, exposing Myra to sudden violence during her formative years. He was a competitive boxer who would also engage in weekend bar brawls.

"He used to beat her a lot," Entwhistle said. "Her father was a very, very powerful influence on her life. She had a tough personality type to start with. If you combine that with a violent childhood, a childhood where she was taught how to be violent, how to be aggressive, then you end up with an unusual personality type."

Myra hated her father and saw him as a bully. He would teach her to box, often hitting her across the head when she performed the techniques incorrectly.

"My father wielded total parental control," Myra said. "I rebelled against it. Fought against it. All my life until I was old enough to free myself from it. All his attempts to control me, even the successful ones were at great cost and were the result of bitter recriminations and often a hard physical punishment."

Myra's father would give her spankings without warning, leaving her buttocks bruised.

Once when she was bullied by a little boy and came home with bruises on her face, her father locked her out of the house. He told her to either face down the bully or he was going to beat her up himself.

"I set up the street to meet my persecutor," Myra recalled. "I quickly concentrated on whatDad had told me and showed me. As Kenny's hand came up, I shot up my left hand, fist bunched towards his head. As I predicted, both hands went up to protect his face and I lifted my right hand and slammed it into his tummy, hitting him hard. With a gasp, Kenny Holden's knees crumbled and before he could recover I slammed my left fist into the side of his head. Kenny was so heavily shocked he sat down heavily on the floor and burst into tears. I stood looking down at him triumphantly."

Myra saw a lot of her father in Ian Brady. Aggressive. Ultra-violent.

"Myra did what we call in psychology, 'transference,'" Orange said. "She saw in Ian what she saw in her father. She never got her daddy's love. So in her mind, she saw Ian as Daddy. She wanted Daddy's love and would do whatever Ian wanted. That was part of her cycle. Transferring a deep need for her father's love onto Ian. There is the strong possibility that had Myra never hooked up with Ian she would have never become a murderer. But the two of them together? Horrific results."

"The bringing together of Myra Hindley and Ian Brady," Entwhistle said. "Unleashed an appalling set of criminal acts."

POLLY IS STILL MISSING

The disappearance of Polly Reede sent the town of Manchester on edge. Things like that simply didn't happen there.

"The fact that children were being abducted and killed," Entwhistle said. "Was incomprehensible to the ordinary man and woman in the street."

Myra would soon find out that Ian's sexual fantasies were not limited to teenaged girls.

He wanted boys too.

Myra would again be a willing accomplice in procuring Ian's second victim. This time, it would be twelve-year-old John Killbride. Myra would befriend the young boy before bringing him to the Moors where he would be sexually assaulted by Brady and later killed.

"I had a terrible feeling something had happened to him," John Killbridge's mother recalled when her son didn't come home from school. "Because he wasn't the kind of boy who would leave home for any reason. He was quite happy and very pleasant, always singing and whistling and I just couldn't see him going anywhere with anyone. Unless it was in an innocent way, somebody wanting to do a job with him or something like that. He'd be enticed into a car that way."

Ian would take photos of the body and burial site. This would become part of their ritual, their ceremony. They would perform the murder then take photographs as if to mark the moment. Then they would return to the scene of the crime days after with their dog "Puppet" in tow. They would take more pictures and relive what took place only days earlier.

"He stopped me as I was walking (to take a picture)," Myra recalled. "And said to turnaround. Moved me about a bit. Told me to kneel down and look at 'Puppet' whose head was showing when he was still wrapped inside my coat. I now know, and knew quite soon afterward, that he photographed me virtually kneeling on John Killbride's grave."

AN INSATIABLE HUNGER

Four months had elapsed between the Pauline and John Killbride murders. But now Ian could not wait long. He ordered Myra to deliver another victim to the isolated Moors.

His name was Keith Bennett. An exuberant, trusting boy, Keith looked like the proverbial nerd with a gap-toothed smile and professorial eyeglasses.

"Keith was a cheeky little lad," Entwhistle said. "He liked to go out and have fun."

Trusting that Myra was taking him some place fun, the young Keith was ambushed by Brady who wrapped a cord around his neck.

Myra did her usual best to remain detached while the horrific attack took place.

"I hadn't wanted this to happen," Myra recalled. "I was tense and terrified. I tried to concentrate my mind miles away from where I was. Finally, after roughly what I think was a half an hour by which time dusk began to descend. I heard him whistle or call. When I stood up, he was waving me back down to the stream bed. Virtually nothing was said as we made our way back except for him saying the spade was hampering him and he'd have to hide it, which he did."

The twelve-year-old Keith, whose entire family was waiting for him at his grandmother's house, never showed up.

His entire family would be traumatized for life.

"I am a mother," Keith's mother, Winnie Johnson said. "It was my first lad and I've got to find him no matter what."

Keith Bennett's body was never found.

"I have nightmares," Johnson said. "I jump in my sleep. It's getting to me now. Because I just can't get him back."

Meanwhile, Myra and Ian would once again take mementos of their time together, taking photos of themselves along the Moors on Keith's fresh grave. Days later, the two would go to St. James Church for midnight mass.

"I retained a warm religious glow," Myra said. "And came out feeling warmed. Not so Ian who took a long swill of whiskey and went to the grave where he casually urinated."

RITUALS

The photos of their time together became an obsession for Ian Brady. He had an automatic camera where he would set the timer and pose for photographs with Myra. In a few of them, they would pose on top of the fresh graves with Ian playfully choking Myra.

"Myra and Ian would often return to the scenes of their crimes," Orange said. "They would take photos of themselves there and relive the thrill of committing the murders."

Over time, however, the photos would not be enough stimulation. They needed something better. Something more visceral.

Sounds.

Ian Brady decided he would record the audio of their next victim being tortured.

That next victim would be ten-year-old Leslie Ann Downey. Myra would befriend and abduct her from the county fairgrounds.

"They would take her back to their home," Entwistle said. "Where he photographed her and recorded her being tortured."

Ian Brady would listen to the audio tape over and over again, closing his eyes and remembering the horrific acts he committed.

Is is the murder of Leslie that Myra would refuse to talk about in interviews.

"There's a tape that isn't what people think it is," Myra said, trying to downplay her own sadism evident in the tapes. "But it's bad. I just hurt so much to think that I've been such a cruel bastard."

THE RUSH OF KILLING

Like a drug addict needing a bigger hit to get high, Brady needed more and more of a thrill for his next murder. He started to get sloppy whereas before his attacks were meticulously planned out.

His next victim would be Edward Evans.

"Edwards was sixteen, seventeen years old," Entwistle said. "And he picked him up in a pub in Manchester."

This would be the first time Ian acted in tandem with Myra to obtain the victim. They enticed the young man to come over to their home and there were witnesses in the pub.

The couple also invited Myra's brother in law, Dave Smith to watch the carnage.

"Smith had no idea what was going on," Entwistle said. "He walked into it totally cold, totally unaware and soon found out that he was involved in the most horrific scene with blood all over the place. A man's head being smashed in."

Smith was appalled, then called the police and told them of the killing.

Police arrived on scene within minutes. They discovered the mauled body of Edwards in a tub. Both Ian and Myra would be arrested.

"It is inexplicable as to why the couple would allow Dave Smith to witness the murder," Orange said. "A part of me thinks that it was part of increasing the thrill. The desire to share what they felt was a special moment with someone else."

A CHILLING DISCOVERY

Investigators would then scour the home, finding one unusual clue that would reveal the goings on of the couple now known in the papers as the Moors Murderers.

They found a left over luggage ticket.

The police would go to the central train station and matched the ticket with a suitcase. Inside, the found something they would never forget.

"They kept trophies in suitcases," Entwhistle said. "In there, of course, was the tape recording of Leslie Ann Downey and that proved what they'd done."

The police would play back the tapes. It churned their stomach to hear the tearful cries of Leslie Ann Downey plead for her life.

"You need to do what he says," Hindley screamed at the little girl. "I told you to shut your face!"

"I want to go home," the little girl pleaded.

"Quiet! Do you not speak English?"

The tape would be played for the jurors at the trial of the couple.

According to witnesses, you could hear a pin drop when they played the tape in court.

"Afterward there was a long, stony silence," Entwhistle said. "As people reflected on what they just heard."

DENIAL

Myra would maintain her own innocence of the murders and repeatedly state that she never witnessed any of the killings herself.

"My solicitor (defense attorney) told me they'd found the body of a child," Myra said. "Identified as Lesley Ann Downey, did I know anything about it? And I said 'No.' A week after that, I'm not sure, they found John Killbride's body and they charged me with, I think it was the murder of John Killbride. Yes, it was.They set me down behind a table and behind it was a large poster of John Killbride. 'Will you just identify these pictures or these photos and tell us if you seen them before.' I'd say, yes, and then they turned over the picture to another photo of the unearthed body of John Killbride."

The picture, Myra would state, made her cry.

LETTERS TO MOMMA

Myra would write her mother numerous letters before her trial. She would order her mother to destroy the letters after she read them but her mother thought otherwise. She would also tell her mother to keep the photographs of her and Ian to herself.

"Don't believe what they're saying about us," Myra wrote. "It is all lies."

But the mothers of all the victims didn't see it that way.

In court, they all had an opportunity to confront Myra.

"The worst part was being confronted by Mrs. West in the witness box," Myra recalled. "And I was looking at her as she was giving evidence and she saw me looking at her and she screamed across at me. 'How can you look at me?' And she called me every name under the sun."

It is at this point that Myra stated that she began to fully realize the gravity of her crimes.

"It suddenly hit me just what I'd done and I think he (Ian) sensed this," Myra said. "We were sitting next to each other and he just put his hand on my arm and squeezed my arm. And I turned around and looked at him, and he was telling me with his eyes to keep quiet."

The jury would find them guilty and in May of 1966 both would be sentenced to life in prison.

STANDING BY HER MAN

Myra refused to testify against Ian. There were some legal experts at the time who believed that if she gave evidence against Brady she would have walked free. But she didn't. She elected to take the punishment along with him.

Instead, she accepted her sentencing and continued to write her mother.

"Dear Mum," Myra wrote. "I knew that I would have to go to prison for some time for 'harboring'. But I didn't think it would be for this long. Ian is in prison, in the special wing. Poor thing, he sews mailbags during the day. He says it helps to pass the time quicker than expected. Will you do one thing for me, ma'am? Take out a policy on me or for me, for a half gram a week. I can't even begin to think of the future. It will be something to fall back on."

"Ian has got a little mouse in his cell. He feeds it crumbs and sits in bed watching it nibble them. The other night, he left it half a chip, thinking it wouldn't touch it but when he woke up the next morning it had disappeared."

Over the next three years, Myra would bombard her mother with requests for the photographs of her and Ian together. She said she did this at the behest of Ian who wanted both the slides and photographs desperately. Myra's mother eventually relented by was sure to allow the police copies of the negatives.

"Ian wanted those pictures back so bad because it reminded him of the events," Orange said. "That is the sort of thing we've come to expect from certain types of serial killers. They want to relive the moment in their fantasy. They'll take mementos, pictures, different elements of their crime in order so they can relive it in their minds. The pictures of Myra holding their dog on those burial sites were of paramount importance to Ian."

Myra would die in prison in 2002 of respiratory failure. Her ashes would be scattered over the Moors, a place that she loved so much.

"Was Myra Hindley sick or was she evil?" Entwhistle asked. "She had a violent father. She met a sexually sadistic man who desperately wanted to be a serial killer. All those things came together and made her carry out some evil, appalling crimes."

Ian Brady remains alive, living out his years under suicide watch in a psychiatric facility where he has repeatedly stated that he will kill himself if given the chance.